THE HAPPY HOMEWORKER

How To Stay Productive, Keep Balanced And Be Fulfilled Working From Home

Nik Haley

First paperback edition May 2020

Cover design by the author in Canva.
Laptop design on front cover and "The Happy HomeWorker" site logo made with logomakr.com.
Author photo: Malcolm Hitch

ISBN 978-1-8380596-4-4 (Paperback)
ASIN B088HJTQL5 (eBook)

Published by
PIXHAM
Books

www.pixhambooks.com

www.thehappyhomeworker.com

Note

The word "HomeWorker" is used throughout. This rather Orwellian neologism is employed to differentiate "home work" from "homework" (of the school variety), and is catchier than "someone who works from home"!

Free Gift

I've prepared a helpful FREE cheat sheet for you: **"20 HomeWorking Tips to Supercharge Your Day"**. To get yours, follow this link to the Happy HomeWorker website:

www.thehappyhomeworker.com/20tips

You'll also find other freebies, resources, blog posts and helpful information all about HomeWorking.

Disclaimer

The advice and opinions I give in this book are mine alone and are borne out of a career spent working from home, trying to figure out the best ways to make it work for my family, myself, and my career. I give no guarantees that what works for me will work for you. But I do suggest trying it and finding out! Where I give advice about wellbeing, mental health, fitness and diet, please remember that I am a professional composer and writer, not a medical professional, nutritionist, personal trainer or life coach.

You're here because you want some perspectives and advice on working from home and how to make it work for *you*. Everyone's different, but we're also all the same. I've tried to take my experience of what works and tailor it to suit many different kinds of HomeWorker.

Dedication

For my wife Becky, for your years of accepting my career, dealing with its ups and downs and being a rock of support through everything.

And to my two brilliant children (whom I was homeschooling throughout the majority of the period spent writing this book), I say thank you for sometimes letting Daddy work, and for giving me — on a daily basis — the opportunity to prove the efficacy of the coping strategies recommended herein!

CONTENTS

1. An Introduction to **HomeWorking**

HomeWorking is huge right now. It's also known as "WFH" (work from home), telecommuting, remote working, flexi-working and mobile working. Increasing numbers of people every year are beginning to explore the possibility that they can earn their living from the comfort of their own home.

Some manage to wangle the ability to remote work in their current job, splitting their time between home and the office. Others quit their jobs and begin a brand new journey in one of the many possible HomeWorking careers.

And a growing section of the population — young people — never actually begin a conventional job, instead turning to the vast, open frontier of internet businesses which allow them to HomeWork.

HomeWorking's great, a dream come true. Until it isn't.

Because the truth is, whatever kind of work you choose to do from home, you're going to face some pretty enormous challenges in actually making it work for you. Those of us who've experienced HomeWorking know it can be every bit as difficult, if not more so, than working in an office or other workplace.

This book will teach you how to make HomeWorking work for you.

> *Just for absolute clarity: "HomeWorking" has nothing to do with homework, as in the stuff school kids do. Just getting that out of the way.*

If you're sick of seeing books and videos about what jobs you *could* do from home and instead, want to learn what you do **once you've picked one**, this book is for you. I'm here to offer support, advice and countless hacks developed over twenty years of HomeWorking.

It's a success manual and survival guide for anyone who does anything to make money from home, including:

- Entrepreneurs
- Remote workers/telecommuters
- Parents juggling career & kids at home
- Retirees supplementing their pensions
- Students with a side hustle
- Professionals self-isolating in times of illness
- Artists/musicians/writers/creatives
- YouTubers, bloggers, influencers, social media managers & other e-freelancers
- Remote salespeople
- Virtual travel agents
- Virtual assistants
- Online educators

- ...and anyone else whose career allows them to work from home, or anywhere else!

You're Going to Learn:

- How to beat procrastination and make your productivity skyrocket.
- How to juggle everything & separate your home and work life to find balance
- The importance of looking after your wellbeing.
- How to avoid overwhelm, burnout and stress.
- How to be a good boss and employee — because you're both!
- How to build a daily routine that works for you.
- How to approach working from home with kids around.
- Diet tips centred around healthy home cooking.
- Exercise tips for easy, short workouts.
- How to set goals, track progress and hold yourself accountable.
- How to develop a HomeWorker mindset.
- How to plan & structure your days to make the most of your work hours.
- How to build winning habits that become second nature.

We'll focus on how you're going to take responsibility for yourself, placing equal emphasis on your career success *and* your wellbeing and happiness.

At the end of each chapter are key **Takeaways** that sum up the key messages, and **MiniWins** — exercises that empower you to take charge of finding the right path for your HomeWorker life.

Have a Notebook and Pen Ready

Many of the MiniWins involve you writing things down, so I'd recommend you **have a notebook handy** to jot down the Takeaways and complete the MiniWin exercises. Once you've read the whole book and completed all the MiniWins, you'll have a personalised compendium of thought experiments, brainstorms, goals, charts and lists to which you can refer whenever you're in need of inspiration.

Pros & Cons of HomeWorking

If you're committed, willing to work hard and — crucially — once you've chosen the right goals to work towards, then making your living from home can be every bit as rewarding as a traditional "job" and every bit as lucrative, sometimes more so.

There's a wealth of interest in what kind of jobs you can do from home and reams of online content about it. But there's far less content devoted to *how* you should approach doing them — how you're going to fit the work around your life; how to be productive when you work for yourself; how to stay motivated; how to tackle the inherent drawbacks; how to be **happy** doing this work.

HomeWorking can bring you all kinds of benefits, like:

- Freedom from colleagues distracting you
- No horrible bosses
- Managing your own time. Feeling unwell? No problem, take a sick day. Want a vacation? Sure, you got it!
- You can work in your PJs (but you shouldn't!)

- Your home is your castle, so you can build an environment you *want* to work in
- No commute

However — there's a flip-side to each of these benefits:

- Isolation. No friendly colleagues to chat with or bounce ideas off
- No boss to guide and inspire you, or tell you what to work on next
- You have to manage your own time, which can be daunting, especially if you have to juggle other commitments or have kids.
- Working in your PJs is a nice thought, but eventually you just want to feel a bit more…professional. And smell better.
- Your home might be your castle, but it's also your home! It can be really hard to separate your work and home life, especially if you don't have much space.
- No commute means no period of separation between work and home. No train ride on which to read books, or to stare out of the window and do some deep thinking.

To put it another way: the grass isn't always greener.

And there are more drawbacks too: no pension, no healthcare, no bonuses, no incentive schemes, no holiday or sick pay, no hierarchical structure within which to work (or through which to rise up) and no work social events — though some may regard this as a plus!.

There's no accounts department, no marketing, no HR, no sales. You're the head of all of these departments when you HomeWork.

Loneliness is real for some, and hard to handle. Being responsible for *everything* can overwhelm you. Getting started can be tough, and finishing projects can be impossible. Handling the distractions of a busy home life can be frustrating.

You must have an awareness of these potential downsides. But if you're prepared to put into practice the strategies in this book, you can save yourself time, stress and heartache.

So, if you're serious about taking the plunge (or you have already), then let's dive in!

Before we begin, a note about money.

Getting Rich

This book won't make you rich. But you knew that.

Very few books can, despite what many promise. And those that can only do so insofar as they elicit well-informed action from you.

As far as I can tell, there are only three ways to be wealthy:

1. Be born into a rich family and inherit your wealth
2. Win the lottery
3. Earn lots of money by working at something and being tremendously successful

Now we can go ahead and assume that no.1 hasn't happened and that no.2 is unlikely to. Well, I hope you also know that no.3 isn't guaranteed either.

That's just fine. Because my goal isn't to make you rich; it's to help you be productive, balanced and happy. Specifically, my goal with this book is to help you find daily contentment and success in your HomeWorking life. Success here doesn't just mean "raking in money". In this book, I use the word success to describe the feeling of having accomplished a goal, of staying balanced in your life, of being happy with your work and having the sensation that your day was spent doing something worthwhile, something that *means* something.

Now it could be that once you've put into practice the advice given here, that you go on to huge financial success — and perhaps I will in part have helped towards that end — but I really hope you're happy and content when you get there. And then you can look me up and buy me dinner or a house or something — I mean, fair's fair.

This Isn't a Jobseeker's Guide

If you're someone who picked this book up because you're *interested* in working from home, I invite you to Google "work from home" and see just how many blogs, books, YouTube videos, online courses and websites there are, devoted to all the possibilities out there to make your living from your home. Not all of them are legitimate, so do use caution and watch out for the charlatans, but lots of the content on this subject truly does present some *fantastic* opportunities. After your Google search, come back here and learn the stuff they won't tell you about the reality of actually chasing those opportunities!

There are so many jobs HomeWorkers do, and more are being invented every day. The jobs themselves are somewhat outside the scope of this book, so we're going to set aside the specifics of *what* you'll be HomeWorking at and focus on the *how*.

N.B. Not everyone who "works from home" actually works at their house. Coffee shops, libraries, bookstores and parks across the globe are full of laptop warriors. They're smashing out their side hustle in between lectures, they're checking their affiliate marketing ledgers before taking the kids to school, or they're writing the third draft of their novel in between getting the car cleaned and picking up dry cleaning. For these people, (some of whom couldn't *bear* to work at their house and simply "must get out and about"), the vast majority of the principles and advice in this book will still apply.

Ditto for part-time remote workers, who split their working time between home and the office.

So let's assume you've chosen a career (or careers) and are either working from home already, or you're close to going for it.

You Don't HAVE to HomeWork!

If it's in your power to decide whether or not you work from home, and if you're struggling to see how it will work for you, then don't feel you have to. It's not for everyone, to be sure. If you're unsure, maybe it would be worth dipping your toe in by trying some part-time HomeWorking, if possible? However, if you're someone who prefers going out to a job and having that separation between work and home, then more power to you.

If you decide against committing to HomeWorking, you may still want to read on, to help with those times when you *have* to work away from your usual workplace, say because of health issues, an office refurbishment, or a work trip.

But do give HomeWorking a try if it's something you're considering.

It will be tough, especially if you haven't done it before. But like anything, once you become accustomed to the challenges and make the necessary adjustments to your working day, you may well find it's the best thing you ever did.

Takeaways

- HomeWorking's potentially fantastic, if you do it well
- HomeWorking has many downsides, so you need to be prepared
- There are countless different HomeWorking jobs you can do but very little in the way of support for how best to do them
- HomeWorking may not be for you, and that's OK!

MiniWin: List Out Your Challenges

In your notebook, write a list of all the things that you're most worried about when it comes to working from home, or are already finding challenging if you've begun already. Just writing them down will help clarify your thinking about the ways in which each issue affects you, and what you need to see change in order to improve the situation.Next to each one, write what would need to be the case or what needs to change in order for you *not* to consider it a downside.

Well done! You've defined the scope of any issues you're facing. That's an important first step.

Now you can tackle each one in turn. Hopefully, you'll find lots of answers in this book!

Some of the things will involve changes that you can make; some will involve communicating with others to encourage them to make changes, others you will have no control over but can find ways of coping with.

So...you're going into HomeWorking with your eyes open wide. Now let's talk about what I can do to help.

2. My HomeWork: Why This Book?

I've been a HomeWorker pretty much my entire career. I do it well now, I didn't always. I want to help you do it well too. I'm going to give you my tried and tested methods for HomeWorking that will keep you productive, balanced and happy.

So a very brief bit of background: **I'm a Composer.**

The vast majority of us composers are HomeWorkers. Except we don't call it "home" when we're speaking to clients. We don't say "I work from home," or "I'm in the office today." No, we say, "I'm in the studio." Even if it's based in a bedroom, it's our studio. The living room might be awash with a tangled spaghetti of cables and the heat of a thousand blinking LEDs of our Fancy Composing Studio Equipment (or "gear"), so it's not the living room we're working in, it's our **studio.** *Got it?*

Early Days

I longed to call myself a composer for many years, but the truth is, I spent my twenties doing anything and everything I could lay my hands on (that was even vaguely connected to music) to pay the rent. At the time, that wasn't composing. I worked lots as Youth Musical Theatre Practitioner. Mostly this meant teaching kids songs from the shows, but it did also lead to some great nitty-gritty theatrical devising work, creating new musicals and working with various youth organisations to benefit the lives of underprivileged kids by using their expressive skills like rap, drumming, songwriting, beat making, DJing, street dancing, poetry writing to make a piece of musical theatre that told their story and empowered them to perform it. I co-owned and ran a theatre company for a while, and worked for many more including British Youth Music Theatre, National Youth Music Theatre, The National Theatre Learning and others.

Though a lot of this work was practical and not home-based, a large portion of my time was spent HomeWorking since I had to spend time planning lessons, preparing music and constantly hunting for the next paid gig, all from my computer at home.

It was a time of great work, great experiences, and no money.

Getting Serious

In my thirties, I got married, had kids, bought a house…and so, of course, I got serious about income. I ended up building a lucrative career working for a choir company as a leader of five choirs, totalling over 600 people. It was a fantastic experience and allowed me to create my own workshop, where I combined choirs with a full symphony orchestra and toured that workshop across the entire UK. On top of all that, I then became a Regional Brand Manager for the company.

This work wasn't sustainable long-term because I was essentially working three jobs. I would spend every day in my studio HomeWorking: communicating with my team of other choir leaders, taking care of all the admin for the choirs and the workshops, which involved emailing members, planning shows, speaking with venues, taking bookings for the workshops, maintaining the website, creating teaching resources for the workshop, promotion, advertising and a host of other duties. But then, I would kiss my wife and young son goodbye and go out for the evening to rehearse, to lead a performance, to a workshop. Often, I'd work weekends too.

I was earning six figures by now, in the music industry. Great! Yet, I was working so much that my work/life balance was awful. I had little to no downtime, and even when I did get to hang out with my wife and two-year-old son, I was usually always aware of the mountain of work waiting in the wings for me, so I couldn't fully relax. I felt it, and so did they. Oh, and did I mention, we renovated an old house during this period?! Oh, and did I also mention that my wife was expecting our daughter in the exact same period?

It was a time of great success in my career, combined with great pressure and stress at home. Mercifully, it was short-lived and I was able to put changes in place before any long-term ill-effects were felt.

Now, working from home with under 5s around is a challenge, but the positive is that you can see a lot of them throughout the day. Both my kids have had lots of Daddy time, certainly more than if I'd been commuting to a 9-5. But I knew that if this career of mine continued beyond them starting school, that I'd be in danger of missing bedtimes as I went out to rehearsals. And seeing as I worked all day before that, I'd hardly see them during the week. This thought was unconscionable.

Also, I wasn't writing any music!

Something had to give.

Refocus

That was when I decided to drop everything and focus on composing, just composing. Which pretty much meant starting over. It's hard walking away from six figures. My guess is that some of you on the HomeWorking journey will have been in the same position before taking the plunge to work for yourself. It's scary suddenly not having an income, especially one you've gotten used to. It puts pressure on your partner (if they work) and pressure on you. But it still felt good, because this was *my* pressure.

So I began composing music for TV, adverts, online, anyone who'd give me a gig. I've since had some success in that area, but nothing like what I was earning before. It's brought me pride, work I love doing, and, of course, I get to keep HomeWorking. And now that I'm able to plan my hours myself again, I can find time for writing. Which makes me happy. Which makes me a better composer, a better husband, and a better father. I do the kids' school runs, clubs and meals during the week, and we're joined by Mummy (who works normal hours in an office) for a good amount of time in the evenings and all weekend.

So the balance is better. Not perfect, but certainly a vast improvement on before.

Side Note: I don't think anyone can make their life exactly balanced and perfect day in day out, can they? There are plenty of books out there telling you that you can, but I maintain a healthy scepticism about that. The modern world isn't really geared towards us feeling that way, is it? But I think that striving for *enough* balance is…enough. And learning to keep perspective.

So, now I'm an actual, professional Composer. There, I said it, feels good.

However...

I still don't seem to be able to commit to it as a full-time career. There are a few reasons:

1. I've always been a "Slashie"

Before it became a trendy word for Millennials with Slash/Slash jobs, I was working in multiple fields (most composers do). I've been a Singing Tutor/Musical Director, a Youth Theatre Practitioner/Musical Theatre Deviser, an Orchestrator/Arranger, a Record Producer/Songwriter, a Choir Master/Manager/Conductor/Workshop Leader, a Composer/Writer, and many of these in combination.

So accustomed to the life of a Slashie have I grown that I can't imagine not working in this way. So naturally, after spending a few months writing music for library albums and working on client commissions, going back and forth on edits, and just "doing" composing, I'm ready for some writing. That's how my fiction novel has been written, as a side project to cleanse my palette whenever composing work gets too samey. But then, once I've spent long enough away from my DAW (Digital Audio Workstation: it's the app we composers use to make and record music on our computers), I'm itching to compose music again.

Others may long to just do one thing, one perfect, life-affirming thing that's their dream career. And that's fine. But for me at least, once a Slashie, always a Slashie.

2. I'm not always full-time

Fitting in a working day in between school runs is a challenge. If you're serious about getting more work done without it affecting your family life, you're going to have to a) have an honest conversation with your partner about when it might be acceptable to work in the evening after the kids are in bed, or b) get up early.

This suits me fine, but it does rather mean that there are limits to the music projects I can take on. The TV music world, for example, operates on a last-minute, we-need-this-yesterday basis. Music's usually one of the last things to be added to any production before its release, and the time constraints can be very demanding. I've had several commissions that have required me to essentially give my life over to that project until the deadline is met. It's fine to work that way once in a while (and actually quite exciting), but to do it any more than I do would start to seriously affect mine and my family's hard-won life balance.

3. The music industry isn't always a great place to work

Having dipped my toes in, I'm not entirely comfortable in the music industry. I'm happy splashing around in the shallows, but I wouldn't want to become submerged in that ocean. Not least because in the music industry, there really are sharks out there, I've met some! (If we ever meet socially, ask me to tell you the story of my brief career as a pop music producer).

But seriously, it's famously not a great industry for promoting the mental health of those who work within it. I'm not saying every member of the music community isn't happy and fulfilled; there are some wonderful folks around, and I've had the pleasure of working with lots of them. But the sharks are always there. And not just sharks: there are piranhas, who want to nibble away at your talent, leeches who want to feed off your work, and narcissistic jellyfish, who will sting you hard if you cross their path.

So I've accepted, not altogether reluctantly, that there are waters in which I shan't be swimming as a composer.

And that's just fine, because...

4. There are other things I love doing

Writing, for one. Over the last twenty years I've written scripts for musicals, screenplays, TV shows and novels. Some have seen the light of day, others have been pet projects, but there's always been a pull to write. I also wanted to write books that help people, specifically ones that get them towards achieving some kind of balance in life.

So...I Wrote This Book For You!

When I looked into writing a nonfiction book, I obeyed the old maxim of "write what you **know**," and the newer (less catchy) one of "write what you know can **serve** people and add **value** to their lives." Well, it was a no-brainer. If there's one thing I know, one thing I have accidentally learned over the course of my twenty-year varied career, it's how to HomeWork!

Through many years of trial and error, mistakes and successes, distractions and temptations, I've developed routines, productivity hacks and self-care strategies that have helped me not only to cope but to thrive working from home. And they'll help you too.

As more and more of you take the HomeWorking plunge — excited by whatever business, opportunity or passion you've committed to — you need to consider how this *huge* life change is going to affect you, your family, your work and your home. The benefits are great but can only be appreciated if you know how to handle the challenges.

Whether you're a budding online marketer, a YouTuber, starting your e-commerce business, writing a novel or *anything*, I'll share the tactics of how to set up your days and weeks, so you can work like a top HomeWorker, and stay relaxed and happy while you do!

So, by all means, go check out another "5 Steps To Financial Freedom Working From Home!" video on YouTube. Then, if you're actually going to follow the advice in it and start your HomeWorking journey, come back and read this book, because you're gonna need it!

I can't promise you that whatever career you choose to work from home at will be a success (nor can anyone, no matter what those videos say), but what I can definitely do is help you make your HomeWorking life work for you, maximising your chances of success and making sure you don't lose yourself along the way.

Takeaways

- There's more to working from home than just the work you do.
- HomeWorking brings along with it an entirely new set of challenges to surmount and problems to solve.
- I've done it the wrong way and the right way. The right way's better for your work, your happiness and your sanity!

MiniWin

Write down a few interests and hobbies that you enjoy outside of "work".

Is there a way to incorporate any of them into your business model?

The answer may well be "no," and that's fine. However you may hit upon something that can spark your passion *and* become a part of your HomeWorking life.

3. HomeWorker Balance

Finding the right balance of work and home life is one of the most important and difficult tasks we all face, no matter where we work.

But HomeWorkers are brought face to face with the contrasts, crossovers and conflicts between the two worlds on a daily basis.

You must work where you live. Where you eat, sleep, rest, convalesce when sick, play, argue, dream…the whole gamut of emotions we feel in life is, at some point, felt at home. When you have to go to a workplace, these facets of your life can encroach and raise their heads at inconvenient times, to be sure. However, for the most part, there is an automatic separation that exists between your two worlds, which makes it easier to mentally shift gears when at work.

Not so at home. This is your base, your fox hole, your cubby, your den. This is your centre, your protection. As soon as it has to also become a place where work is done, that dynamic will instantly shift, and your balance will be potentially destabilised.

And it's not just your balance. There are the *other people*.

Living With Others

These are the ones whose home this is, but whose office it ain't, like a loved one or partner with whom you live, or perhaps you have roommates. To some degree at the very least, your work is also going to become a part of their home life. And they may not feel altogether happy about that. They may not even have had a say.

You're going to need to take their point of view and any objections they have into account to try to maintain balance for all.

You may even cohabit with another HomeWorker. Though there will be a higher degree of understanding given your shared experience, there will, nonetheless, be as strong a need to cooperate, communicate and compromise accordingly.

Living Alone

Though it may not be your preference or life goal to live alone, if you're a HomeWorker who does, you should rejoice in one thing: you can skip all this potential hassle and just 'do you'.

There will still, however, be a need to find balance in your own life between work and home. And you may find that the lack of people around you is all the more isolating, given that you already work alone. In these cases, it's all the more important to get off-site as often as possible, to reach out to friends and family and even to other HomeWorkers (via social media groups, forums etc) in order to remember that, though it may feel like it, you're not alone.

Before I continue, I'm going to share with you this account of when my family and I had to stay home and try to live and work together full-time. It was an education in finding balance, to be sure! Not only did I have to find a compromise between my own work and my home, but also fit both around the work and home lives of three other people: my wife and two children!

Case Study: Coronavirus — **When HomeWorking Went Global**

I started writing this book in the weeks before the coronavirus (COVID-19) pandemic began in 2020. Little did I know when I started that I'd be tapping into a topic that millions would soon be dealing with, many of them against their will.

As more and more people in countries all over the world were asked (or told) to self-isolate and work from home, as the offices closed and the roads and train platforms emptied, more people than ever before began to experience the joys and challenges of HomeWorking.

Many hated it and couldn't *wait* for life to return to normal, but many others got bitten with the HomeWorking bug and began to explore how they could turn this temporary state of affairs into a long-term reality.

And they all learned the need to put into place strategies and approaches that they'd never thought about before.

How My HomeWorking Life Changed

It didn't, at first. I just kept going as usual as more and more people began self-isolating. While all these people were experiencing huge upheaval in their lives, I felt lucky that for all the hassles it's caused me over the years, my experience HomeWorking was now going to stand me in good stead and would mean I wouldn't suffer as much disruption as others.

But then *everyone* was sent home from work.

My wife works in an office for a large company who had rightly asked all their employees to HomeWork. Being suddenly faced with this massive life change was daunting for her.

But we were in a fortunate position in one sense: she had a husband who could offer first-hand advice on how to handle HomeWorking, and I had someone with whom I could conduct extra research for this book, seeing first-hand the challenges and solutions that someone faces when they transition from a regular 9-5 to HomeWorking. It was nice seeing more of each other, and we achieved a new balance fairly swiftly.

But then…they shut the schools! Everyone was asked to remain at home for the foreseeable future.

So now, like millions of other people across the planet, we had two adults working from home and two children who needed caring for, educating and entertaining every day. Our kids are 4 and 7.

This was going to be hard.

But I felt like it was the perfect time to put all the advice I'm giving about work/life balance through its paces…and *really* stress test it.

Here's my account from the early days of our family being under the same roof permanently, which was published as a blog post on The Happy HomeWorker Blog in March 2020.

How to Cope With Life During the Coronavirus Lockdown

This is it.

There are now four people in the house. All day long. Every day.

Two kids sent home from school.
One Mum forced to HomeWork by her corporate employer.
And me: a HomeWorking Dad used to having the place to himself.

Welcome to Coronavirus Purgatory.

This is the New Normal. For now, at least. It's designed to keep us and others safe. So we need to accept that it's going to be challenging and knuckle down to making the best of it.

Well, let's get on with it then…

The House

Your house is about to learn how to multi-task as an office, school, gym, playroom, cinema and home.

Make sure your living space is set up for its new use as far as you can. Obviously, there's not a lot you can do with a two-bedroom apartment, but you can still make use of the space by tidying away non-essential items and leaving maximum workspace on the dining table, for example.

In our case, home is a 3-bedroom Victorian semi-detached cottage. Which means that for four people, it's small. And it's now the permanent host of two careers and the education and playtime of two children, as well as its usual duty as "family home".

Its one saving grace is it enjoys a large garden with a garden office: Daddy's workspace.

Obviously, the kids' playtimes will often be spent together, but they need their own spaces too, especially for school work. And their taste in TV shows has begun to diverge.

There's a small basement room (another plus) — the seven-year-old's hovel, with myriad activities, toys, a TV and desk. So he's sorted. The four-year-old uses the living room above, which essentially consists of a second TV, sofa and small dining table used for mealtimes, baking, Play-Doh, colouring, writing and about a thousand other things.

That's a four-year-old's space now, leaving Mummy with few options for a quiet workday.

The solution? She's set herself up in our son's bedroom, since he has a desk as part of his cabin bed. So that space is now bedroom by night, office by day. Re-purposing bedrooms is one way you can make the most of space, especially if you need somewhere to be away from others and make calls.

So during the day, all four of us have access to at least two separate spaces:

	Main Space	**Secondary Space(s)**	**Extra Space**
7 year old:	Basement	Living Room (for family time)	Garden
4 year old:	Living Room	Her bedroom	Garden
Mummy:	Son's Bedroom	Our bedroom / Kitchen	Garden
Daddy:	Garden Office	Our bedroom / Kitchen	Garden

In the evening, the main living space becomes home to all four of us, as usual. Mummy and Daddy enjoy cooking so the kitchen is a relaxing space whilst the kids chill in the living room, then we join them in there for Family Movie Night (which usually lasts 30 minutes to an hour before bed).

By night, everything returns to normal as the kids go to bed and the living room is used once more as a Grown-Up Space, with Netflix and Conversation and Calm.

Once you've got your new configuration of rooms sorted and moved furniture around as needed, it's time to make a plan for how you're going to cope with the new arrangements.

The Best-Laid Plans...

You've gotta have a plan. Even if it only lasts until just after breakfast, you've gotta have a plan.

But there will be times when everything just goes wrong.

The kids will choose the wrong moments to erupt into noisy disagreements just when one of us is in the middle of some intense work, or on a call. Both adults will feel the frustration of not having complete control over their workdays. The kids will get cabin fever, especially if the weather prevents them from going outside.

The best thing you can do is to accept that you cannot change this fact.

Of course, it's not an ideal arrangement. If it were, this is how all families would operate. There are times when it's going to suck.

But we have to make the best of it and try to be patient with each other. The kids, in particular, deserve a stable, happy environment, so it's important to remember to approach all challenges and bumps on the road with a degree of perspective, and what we in the UK refer to as a "Dunkirk spirit".

Approach each frustration with stoicism if possible. Remember why this is happening, and if you and your family are healthy, be grateful for that instead of focussing on the difficulties of the situation.

Working Arrangements

You'll need to work these out based on your family's unique situation. In ours, Mummy's the one with a very successful career, so her job takes priority over my more flexible, HomeWorking one. This, in turn, means I take point with the kids from 9-5.

If both parents have broadly similar income levels, you'll need to share responsibility out more evenly, maybe one of you takes point in the morning, one in the afternoon.

The Daily Routine

Routine is vital.

Having a routine means everyone understands what's expected of them at all times of the day.

It doesn't mean everything's planned out to the minute, and where the kids are concerned, a rough structure works best, one that can ebb and flow to a degree, but puts similar activities at the same time every day.

This is especially important during the week. We're mimicking the school day as far as possible.

Mornings are best for kids' learning and concentration, as we know. Then afternoons are when they need to get their energy out and have lots of playtime!

Example Routine

Here's a rough outline of how we're making it work during the week:

5 am Daddy gets up and gets 2-3 hours work in.

7 am Kids are up and watching TV in their pyjamas, Mummy wakes.

8 am Daddy exercises, everyone has breakfast.

9 am Mummy starts her workday.

9-12 pm Daddy structures school work activities for the kids to do in their separate workspaces and goes between them, monitoring and coaching them.

12 pm All meet up for lunch. Mummy will usually exercise over lunch at work, so she'll keep this going now. The kitchen has the most space for an exercise mat, so now it doubles up as the gym!

1-5 pm This is less structured "free play" time for the kids. They will play games, craft, colour, have garden fun and chill. During this time, Daddy will head back to the garden office, but will still "take point" on the kids, especially when they're in the garden, or if Mummy's work is very intense. But where she can, Mummy will set the kids up with more activities, solve any disputes, etc. If they've had a busy enough morning, they'll usually be happier to be a little more independent during this period, allowing both adults to get some work done.

5 pm Mummy's off the clock, and we all meet up and it's business-as-usual: dinner, baths, movies, games, bed.

7-10 pm Either the grown-ups will relax together, or Daddy might head back to the office for a bit to catch up on work time he missed during the day.

Make Sure Everyone's Day Stacks Up

So here's what everyone's getting in the daytime:

Mummy — a full working day, albeit with the odd interruption.

Pro: She can build in exercise to her day more easily than at work.

Con: Her office space is a seven-year-old's bedroom. She'll need to 'get off site' to stay sane.

Daddy — a mixed-up day, but that's not so different from normal.

Pro: With the time I save on the school run, I might be able to get almost as much work done as a regular school day. This depends on the kids' behaviour and willingness to play independently at times!

Con: Let's not kid ourselves; "taking point" on the kids is going to be challenging some days!

Kids — School work, playtime, relaxing time. Being in their home, which is a safe space.

Pro: Lots of exposure to Mummy and Daddy.

Con: Not much interaction with kids their own ages, except each other.

Getting Outside

The kids' usual week is fairly packed with after school clubs: piano, gymnastics, swimming and dance lessons. They've all been put on hold, so there's going to be a need to find things into which we can plough the children's boundless energy levels.

On fine weather days, the garden will be vital for the kids — for exercise, a change of scene, fresh air, activities, and when Mummy has Had Enough of the Noise.

The usual summer holiday activities will be deployed in full force: nature hunts, camping, roasting marshmallows over a fire bowl, building obstacle courses. We have a hammock, giant cushions, and even a small bouncy castle with a fan that plugs into the office's power supply.

The kids are going to be fine. When the weather's good.

But getting outside just became imperative for the adults too.

I do the school runs, so I get out and about to two different schools twice a day. Plus, most days, I do a run around the local park. So I'm usually OK in terms of daily changes of scene.

But Mummy's a different story. Without her usual commute and the social office environment to which she's grown accustomed over a fifteen-year career, she's going to potentially struggle. She'll be cooped up in her son's bedroom for much of the day; then when the workday ends, she'll be instantly back in her family home, surrounded by the three of us.

The solution we've discussed is that once a day, she gets out of the house and does a "fake commute". This could be a walk, a run or a drive. She can listen to music, have space to think, and just be her for a bit.

This delineation between work and home life is something everyone who works away from home has, and whilst many will enjoy skipping the boredom and rigmarole of the daily commute, they will also miss this side of it.

Ten Tips to Make it Work

1. Adapt your living space to suit everyone's needs, moving furniture if needed.
2. Make sure everyone knows what the schedule is and what's expected of them.
3. Be sure to mix up the kids' day, let activities flow, but have a gentle schedule.
4. Do school work in the mornings, "free play" in the afternoons.
5. Be patient. Respect each others' boundaries and have agreed work times.
6. Build in "off-site" time for everyone if possible.
7. Adults need to communicate, accept the new challenges and be prepared to adjust the arrangements to iron out any problems that arise.
8. Practice stoicism: accept what you can't change and breathe through frustrations.
9. Get outside to a garden or park as often as possible.
10. Embrace the positives! Enjoy the new experience as far as possible.

How long will this last?

At this point, we don't know.

So we have to make life bearable in the meantime.

Let's all stop lamenting the loss of our "normal life" and embrace a bit of change. It's as good as a rest, you know!

Alongside the challenges, there will be plusses. Those of you who work and wish you saw more of your kids in the week are about to *really* have your wishes granted! Those who hate the commute? It's gone!

It's going to be a time where families can really hunker down, re-connect and strengthen their bonds. That's no bad thing.

And through all the inevitable struggles this will bring, just remember one thing:

This won't go on forever.

Unless you want it to...perhaps you'll get a taste for this new life and begin working from home and homeschooling your kids?

Hmm. This won't go on forever!

(Originally published on The Happy HomeWorker Blog, *March 2020)*

Takeaways

- No matter how challenging your work/home set up is — or becomes — there are things you can do to mitigate the stresses and strains that come with trying to balance it all.
- Communicate. Collaborate on a schedule and, where kids are concerned, be willing to drop everything and just play.
- If your priorities need to shift temporarily, then so be it. Agility and adaptability are strengths!

MiniWin

Think of something to which you ordinarily attach a large degree of importance in your work. Now imagine you can't do it anymore because of one of the following reasons:

- You kid just fell over and needs caring for and patching up.
- You need to cook dinner for everyone.
- Your brother is on an important call and needs you to walk his dog.
- You have to do an online food shop for your elderly parents.
- Your kids are asking to play a game with you.

Now…think about how important that thing you were doing *really* is.

Each of these interruptions and distractions forces you to prioritise things other than your work. And that's no bad thing, generally. Not when you gain some life perspective as a result. Nothing is more important than caring for your loved ones, is it? That, to a large degree, is what your work is about in the first place.

So in times of upheaval when your usual nose-to-the-grindstone work ethic is usurped by other circumstances, instead of throwing your hands in the air, take my advice and skip the exasperation and indignation. Instead, use the experience to reboot your thinking about what's truly important to you.

Then, as and when things do return to normal, you'll go back to your regular routine with a renewed perspective that will only serve to improve your life at home and at work.

Not to mention the gratitude you'll feel to be able once more to knuckle down undisturbed!

4. Build Your HomeWorker Business

In this chapter, we'll look at the process of getting started with a HomeWorking business.

If your HomeWork is part of an existing career, you'll be less concerned about the ins and outs of establishing a business structure, but there are still lessons to be learned in this chapter about project management and how to think through a strategy.

Types of HomeWorker

Because more and more people every year are beginning to work from home, some offices and other workplaces are scaling down. The rise of networked technology has meant that not everyone needs to be physically surrounded by people in order to get their work done, even if those people are working on the same project.

Now we have apps like Skype, Slack, Zoom, FaceTime, WhatsApp, Dropbox…the list goes on. Even a decade ago, many of these were still in their infancy; now it's entirely possible to run a whole business remotely using apps like these.

All kinds of people in all kinds of careers can work from home. Here are just a few examples:

• **HomeWorkers with A Normal Job**. That's right; you can have a job in an office and *still* call yourself a HomeWorker, albeit a part-time one! The HomeWorking revolution has begun to allow more and more people to ask their company to have a little flexibility about where their employees do their work from.

• **Entrepreneurs** of all stripes…with little or no outlay, anyone can start a business now. Whether anyone can grow and sustain that business is another matter, but it doesn't stop thousands from trying every year!

• **Parents** with a few hours spare in between the nursery/school run! These are the Mums and Dads looking to boost their incomes with side hustles. Some of the people in this category have grown very successful, across many niches, including "Mommy bloggers", lifestyle consultants, personal trainers or food writers.

• **Online Marketers**. These folks deal in things like sales funnels, SEO strategies, keyword analysis, lead magnets and conversion rates. They know their onions.

• **YouTubers**. If you're going to be recording videos, then unless you work for a video production company, your boss probably won't want you doing it at work! So full-time YouTubers are, by definition, HomeWorkers. Some can get around a lot, some even make their videos about travel, so they are in a slightly different category. However, a good number of YouTubers shoot their content from their home, or a studio that's part of their home.

- **Creatives**. Artists, Musicians, Crafters, Writers, Authors, Animators...the list goes on. Even if their work takes them out of the house at times, a great deal of it can be done from home.

- **Social Media Consultants**. These folks pretty much just look at Facebook and Instagram all day. So, you know, what most of us do on our breaks, except they get paid to do it.

- ...and **countless** and ever-increasing numbers of jobs that can be done from home!

Once you know what kind of HomeWorking business you'd like to create, you'll need a plan. How are you going to get this business off the ground, especially if you're starting from scratch?

It's daunting at first, but the following pages contain steps you can follow to get things moving.

YOU DON'T HAVE TO SEE THE WHOLE STAIRCASE, JUST TAKE THE FIRST STEP.

Martin Luther King, Jr.

Where to Begin

So imagine you've done it.

You've **quit** the job you hated. You really enjoyed seeing the look on your boss's face.

You **rejoiced** that never again would you have to sell your soul to that company for a measly paycheck that never matched what you felt you were worth.

You've watched **millions** of YouTube videos and online courses about online business, you've fed on the excitement of dozens of people sharing their success stories and telling you just how easy this stuff is.

This is it. Day one of your **New Life Working For Yourself from Home**.

You grab a coffee and fire up the laptop.

OK, **what now?** Let's consult the planner (you were organised and spent the weekend planning out tasks for your first weeks and months).

Right...need a website. Need content for the website. Better write some blog posts. What to write about? Better research topics in my niche. Better put keywords in for SEO. Better watch video on keywords to refresh memory. Ooh look, this one's about keywords on FBA, guaranteed six-figure monthly income...hmm, should probably check that out. Logo! I don't have a logo, must add that to planner. Wait, the FBA guy just mentioned Shopify, I should check that out. Still need a website. Homepage...what do I put on it? Hmm, here's an online course that promises to help me make a stunning website in under an hour, only $29. OK, I'll make that investment. Better make another coffee...

The morning passes, and you've learnt *some* things. But you're still no closer to having actually started, and that website of yours is nowhere to be seen.

And panic begins to set in…

Does this sound familiar? If so, you've experienced what all HomeWorkers face, especially entrepreneurs and startups, and that's the dawning realisation that:

It's all on you.

You are responsible for building your career from scratch.
You manage your time.
You must triage and prioritise tasks.
You must handle your own professional development.
You are the point of contact for your business.
You are the head of IT, accounts, finance, purchasing, sales, marketing and catering.
…and **you** still have to make your own lunch and be on time to pick the kids up later!

If you're not ready to face up to this reality, it's going to come and smack you round the face, especially if you haven't worked for yourself before and are used to the structure and safety of working within a company.
But don't worry, you can handle this!

Once you get your head around the huge responsibility now on your shoulders, you'll soon see that in order to cope with it, you just need to spend some time thinking about the next steps.

We're going to break this first period of time down into three phases, each with set timeframes.

1. The Research Phase (1 week)
2. The Decision Phase (1 week)
3. The Setup Phase (2-4 weeks)

At the end of this six week period, you'll be ready to launch your business. Simple. No excuses, no spending too long researching, no endless honing. Just get started. There'll be plenty of time to hone later.

1. The Research Phase (1 Week)

To avoid overwhelm and a potentially crippling, confused entry into the work of HomeWorking, you need to set out your goals clearly and early on.

Spend your first days and weeks mapping out some clear and actionable, achievable goals that will move the needle on your business. The key thing here is to keep the goal realistic and measurable (i.e., it has an easily-definable outcome).

Start by looking at a few key areas. This is the Research Phase.

This is vital, and will ensure you don't waste your time on an idea that's neither practical nor right for you.

> *Whilst you're in this phase, I heartily recommend Pat Flynn's book* Will It Fly? *It's an in-depth manual for how to test your business idea before you commit to spending time and money on it. It has practical steps you can follow if you want to really go into detail. Just don't spend too long analysing!*

• **Decide on what niche you're going to operate in**. You may know this already, but if not, it's crucial that you understand what industry you're starting out in. It could be in the same industry as your old, regular job, or it could be in an entirely new field. Just make sure you've got a clear idea of your niche.

• **Research your market.** Don't skip this step. Find out who else is in your space, who's doing well and why, which areas of the industry are under-served and which are saturated. Do most people in your niche have a podcast? Do they run a YouTube channel? What do their websites look like?

• **What are people talking about in your niche?** Search social media, groups and forums to see what your potential customers are asking about. If a subject is popular or a problem needs fixing, that's where your business needs to be focussing.

• **What products or services are sold in your niche?** Can you offer something similar?

But beware, you need to break this phase up into achievable tasks, or else you could be lost in the Research Phase forever.

Here are some examples of good goals to start your Research Phase off:

Be Able to Write Your Cocktail Napkin Pitch by the End of Week 1

This is the short, one-sentence mission statement that sums up your business' *raison d'être.* Without this, it's not worth continuing. You need to imagine a billionaire investor coming up to you and asking, "What does your company do?" You need to be able to give that person a 20 second, zingy reply that sums up three things:

1. **What you sell.** These are the products and services you intend to trade, at least to begin with. These can change over time, and obviously, it's better to start small and build from there. Examples might be books and t-shirts, consultancy services, digital training products, online marketing expertise or other physical products.

2. **Who it's for.** You may not know your customer demographic yet, or you may have a sense. Either way, the best way to define who your business is geared towards is to work out what problem you solve: the need you meet, the issue you address, the question you answer. Identify a problem people have, make sure there are lots of people out there asking questions about it, and there you have your answer as to who your business is for.

3. **What makes you different.** You don't have to be totally unique and have a brand new, original business model. You just need to know what will make your business stand out, especially if your market is already crowded (which is not necessarily a bad thing, by the way, as it shows that your industry is popular). One of the things that makes your business different is: you. What skills, messages and stories are you bringing to your brand? Think about what approaches you're going to take that perhaps others haven't yet fully explored?

THE ONE THING YOU HAVE THAT NOBODY ELSE HAS IS YOU. YOUR VOICE, YOUR MIND, YOUR STORY, YOUR VISION. SO WRITE AND DRAW AND BUILD AND PLAY AND DANCE AND LIVE AS ONLY YOU CAN.

Neil Gaiman, Make Good Art

Collate the information you gather in these three areas and shape it all into a snappy two or three sentence pitch. N.B. You don't have to put these three things in order! Practice your napkin pitch. You could rehearse it to yourself out loud, or you could even try it out on a loved one and see what they think.

Example

Here's a cocktail napkin pitch for The Happy HomeWorker:

> *The Happy HomeWorker is a brand that serves people working from home who want to balance their work and home life to maximise their productivity and general wellbeing. We have books aimed at HomeWorkers, and have an online ecosystem that incorporates a blog, online community and website with HomeWorking opportunities and learning resources. We're special because we care just as much about helping people develop happiness and fulfilment as we do about their career success.*

Write Notes on 5 Businesses in Your Niche

You don't need to spend weeks on market research. Just use your search engine and some common sense and find five businesses that are operating in the same industry that you intend to. Then, for each one, simply jot down answers to the following questions:

1. **What do they sell?** Products, services, or both? What seems to be their main focus? What's their best-seller that most of their marketing seems geared towards?

2. **Who and where are their customers?** See who's following them on social media, who's engaging with them, who's buying their stuff.

3. **What could you do better than they are?** Decide right off the bat what things they're already doing that you feel you could do, and perhaps do it

better. You may think they have the market sewn-up and that you can't compete, but the truth is, if someone's enjoying a huge market and serving a large community, it proves there's a market there, and that you could grab a piece of it. Your size isn't a problem either, since you're more nimble and agile when just starting out and are unburdened by the apparatus and systems large companies have in place. You're free to really drill down to a specific market group, find their particular problem and hone your messaging so that it addresses that problem in more detail than anyone else. As Pat Flynn says, "The riches are in the niches," which is a catchy pun, but only if you pronounce it "nitch". We British say "neesh". It's a French word, after all…but you know what they say, itch to their own ;-)

That's it. That's your market research done.

You'll do more as you develop and grow your business, but spending too long on this step now will hamper your momentum in this early stage, and you need to make progress. Having a sense of what five competitors in your space are doing will give you a clear enough idea of the direction you need to be taking.

Use Social Media to Get to Know Your Customers

Remember that Facebook, Pinterest, Instagram and the rest are, on top of everything else, giant search engines. You can use them to find out where your niche lives online. And that's where your customers are.

Decide which social media avenues you want to walk down. I recommend at least one, but I wouldn't do more than two or three in the first stages of your business. Remember, you're also the Social Media Manager, and you don't want to be spending your entire workday sifting through your Content Calendar, posting on Instagram Stories and designing Facebook Ads!

Join two or three Facebook groups related to your niche. Join in the conversation and see what people want to talk about. You'll also see what businesses are being promoted there, either within the group's feed or in the sidebar.

Start an Instagram, Twitter or Pinterest account for your brand and begin posting. This is a 'soft launch' strategy. You might not have anything to promote yet and no content in mind, but you can still start building an online presence. Share others' posts, tweets and pins. This is an achievable side-project that you can do alongside setting up your business, and if you commit to posting regularly, you'll have built up a small audience before you launch your business.

Find What's Selling

Speaking of search engines, online retailers are also search engines. Amazon's one of the biggest. Between Google and Amazon, you can play around with the search bar, seeing what auto-complete options come up when you type in products, services or questions related to your proposed business idea.

For example, let's say you're going to start a blog about snowboarding, and you want to sell boards. You'd begin your market research by typing into Google something like "where to find best snowboards".

I just did, and this is what I saw:

Now, I have no idea what an all-mountain snowboard is, nor indeed a freeride one. But that's what snowboarding customers have been typing into Google, so guess what? If you're in that niche, you'd better be serving that need.

Let's try it in Amazon, this time just typing "snowboard":

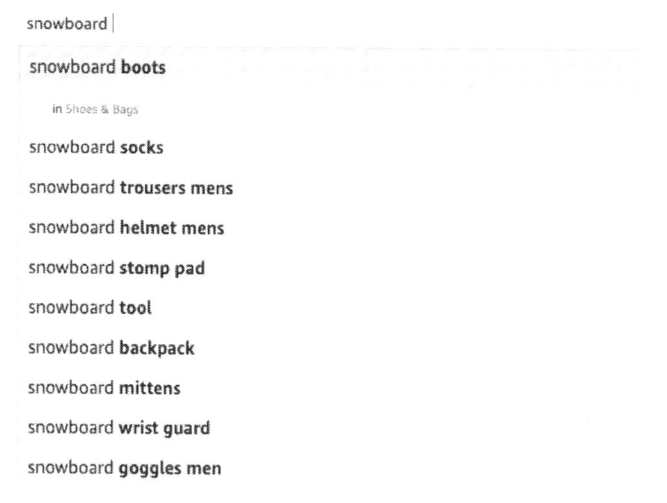

OK, so I'd better find out what the hell a stomp pad is too, then.

Not only will this method point you in the direction of the bestselling products and services in your niche, but it will also give you an idea of what keywords to use when you come to promote things. Knowing which keywords you're serving is vital for your website's SEO (search engine optimisation) and will also be attached to anything you sell via online retailers like Amazon, eBay, and Shopify. Not to mention their importance to online advertising.

> *It's outside the scope of this book to go into too much detail on keywords, so suffice it to say: research this and just be aware of what your keywords are! I would advise typing "keywords and seo for beginners" into YouTube. It's a rabbit hole, to be sure (and what isn't on YouTube?!) but a worthwhile one.*

Once you've played around searching for things, you should have a clearer idea of what's selling well in your niche, and whether you feel you can compete. Perhaps there's something related to these popular products that you feel you could produce better?

Either way, try to find and make notes on up to 10 products and services in your field.

2. The Decision Phase (1 week)

OK, research over. Time to make some decisions.

Take the next week to map out a few things you'll focus on in your business.

Key decisions to make:

Your Product

You already researched products and services that sell in your niche in the Research Phase, so now's the time to choose 1-3 that you'll focus on.

Your Name

You also need a great name. It needs to be catchy and should sum up your business. But don't spend an age on this, just pick one and let's go!

> ***Important:*** *When you've selected a name, do check that its* ***domain name*** *and* ***social media handles*** *are available! For example, before launching The Happy Homeworker, I registered the domain www.thehappyhomeworker.com with Bluehost, and snapped up @thehappyhomeworker on Pinterest, Instagram and Facebook, where I set up both a page and a private group.*

Once you've chosen your name and registered everything you need, you can move on to thinking about branding.

Your Branding

You don't need to spend days and weeks on this. It can change over time, but you will need to at least come up with a decent logo for your business. Use an online design tool like Canva or Logomakr (both free) to create your logo. Decide on your brand's look and colour scheme that you can apply across your website and social media platforms. Have a play and try a few things out. You don't have to commit to a design until the next phase. See what kinds of colour schemes and designs others in your niche are using. The best approach with design, especially if you're not an expert, is to keep it simple and be consistent with the look across all the places where your brand lives online.

Your Ecosystem

This is your business model. Decide if you need a website (you probably do). Will you advertise on social media and/or Google? Will you sell through an online retailer like Amazon or Shopify? Will you promote your services on Upwork and Fiverr? Will you run Facebook Ads? Will your brand have an accompanying content stream like a podcast or a blog?

These are big decisions, but if you've done your work in the Research Phase, you'll already know the answers to most of these questions. Again, see what the competition is doing...if it's working for everyone else, the chances are it will for you too. Try not to be overwhelmed by these decisions. Nothing has to be forever, but you have to start somewhere!

Now the important decisions are made, you can move on to the Setup Phase.

3. The Setup Phase (2-4 Weeks)

By now, you should have a list of things that need building/creating.

For example:

- **Wordpress website**
- **Logo**
- **Blog**
- **Shopify Store**
- **Facebook Group**
- **Instagram account**
- **Content calendar**

Plan out how and in what order you're going to tackle these tasks. For the example above, I would recommend tackling tasks in this order:

- **Logo & branding** - including your slugline and mission statement (remember your cocktail napkin pitch? That!). Time to build the look of your brand. Make logos, banners, backgrounds, you name it. Re-size images to optimise them for each platform (you can find this information out with a quick Google search). Have this all taken care of before you move on to the next step. Your life will be much easier if you have all the design elements ready and waiting with which to populate your website and social media.

- **Website** - keep your web design simple. Don't overreach with fancy plugins, widgets and design elements. A clean, well-organised homepage that sums up your business will suffice in these early stages. You could also consider including the following pages, if appropriate: "About" (that napkin pitch and a bit about you or your company), "Get Started" (where you want your visitors to head first), "Resources" (other products and services you recommend to your customers). You also need to consider putting in a privacy policy, cookie policy, affiliate disclaimer (if you're using affiliate links) and any Terms & Conditions. You also can host your promotional content here (blog, podcast) and have either links to, or embed your commerce store.

> ***Website building.*** *You could pay for someone to do this for you, which needn't cost the earth for a small starter website. But making your own for free is perfectly feasible. The most popular website builder is Wordpress. Wix has a simpler, more graphical user interface, but lacks the range of extra features that Wordpress has. You'll have to decide what's right for you (there are lots of roundups, reviews and comparisons on YouTube).*

- **Shopify Store**. Establish your storefront and add any branding. Add the products you've decided to sell and set your prices.

- **Blog.** There is "How to Launch a Blog" content all over the place that breaks down the steps to starting your own blog, and advises you what to include. It's a massive topic, and one you could spend months learning about. If you're sure you want to go down this road, make sure you have a good few posts written and published before you launch.

- **Set Up Socials.** You'll have already started interacting in Facebook groups in the Research Phase. Now it's time to establish your own Page and Group, keep your Instagram posting schedule up, and build your Content Calendar so you know what subjects you're going to blog/post about and when. Adapt your napkin pitch into short bios for each platform, each of which has different allowances for length and certain conventions (for example, Instagram likes bios with emojis). Putting a call to action in your bio is a great idea, for example, a link to a landing page.

You'll need to plan the above steps according to the business model you've chosen. You can mix and match things, and some projects may require being worked on concurrently. But your aim is to have them all completed **within 2-4 weeks.**

The Next Step

So, if you've been counting, that's 4-6 weeks' work, and you're ready to go! This strategy will get you to the launch. Which is, by definition, only the beginning.

But it's often the hardest stage to get through, so having these concrete steps in place will help you get off the starting line.

What happens after that is will certainly involve lots of trial and error, testing, failures, successes, frustrations, experiments, cul-de-sacs, learning and updating.

Takeaways

- Go through the phases one by one, organising your tasks accordingly: The Research Phase (1 week), the Decision Phase (1 week) and the Setup Phase (2-4 weeks).
- Get to know the market you've selected inside out, decide on your business model, based on what customers in that niche are looking for.
- Build an ecosystem that can serve that need, having all your fundamentals in place before launch.

MiniWin - Launch!

This should really be under the label "MaxiWin".

You don't need to have "finished" everything before you begin putting your business plan into action. There will always be improvements to be made to your systems; things that are working and need expanding, things that have failed and need either ditching or modifying. But getting started — getting to the stage where you've helped your first customer and taken some revenue through the door — will give you such a feeling of pride that you'll gain the motivation to continue down the road you've built and carry on with the hard work.

5. HomeWorker Productivity

This is a huge topic, and one that I've spent twenty years studying.

Productivity is probably the number one practical challenge you'll face in your HomeWorking, especially if you've grown used to a workplace with others around you.

In this chapter, you'll learn:

- How to be both a good boss and a good employee
- How to plan your time efficiently
- How to prioritise and manage tasks and projects using the ADOPTED method
- How to handle interruptions
- The importance of routine
- How to set up your workspace for maximum productivity
- How sleep interacts with your productivity
- Tactics to avoid procrastination
- How to develop discipline and stay motivated

Getting to grips with these techniques will keep you focussed and productive, which is the golden goose for HomeWorkers. You may not have the ability to work the hours you'd ideally like to, so it's important to know how to be as productive as possible during the hours you have.

You're the Boss...*and* the Employee.

This is an important truth to get your head around.

The Boss

Unless you're remote working from your office, the chances are you don't have a boss. In any case, without a boss breathing down your neck, who's going to decide what you should be working on? You are.

If you've never had 'direct reports' working under you before, you may be new to this feeling. It's especially strange for some to realise that they actually *are* in charge. The feeling of responsibility can mess with your mind in several ways.

1. **A feeling of panic.** It's a lot of pressure, and you may not be used to it. However much you hated your boss before, or resented the way the company was run, you usually always knew what was expected of you each day. Which meeting you go to, what your deadlines were, which project to work on, who to speak to and when, what was in your planner, what the chain of command was, and when to stop work for the day. Although you may have a degree of say in *some* of these things when you work for a company, they are largely outside of your control.

This fact (as well as being a source of frustration, for sure) brings with it a kind of comfort, a safety net. You can moan all you want about the Powers That Be, or This Terrible Colleague or Too Many Meetings, but for some people, being handed this structure each day is actually comforting. It's one less thing to worry about. They know their parameters and can just get on with the day. They didn't have to spend time and energy deciding on what to do; someone else did it for them. When this safety net is removed and you realise that *every single decision* is yours to make, it can be extremely daunting, not to mention draining.

2. A power trip. Now, for some people, this realisation that you're completely in charge can bring feelings of elation and relief. It can even become a power trip. It's human nature, especially if you've experienced past resentments towards a boss or a team. You'll say, "I'm free at last! This is the dream! I can work when I want, stop working when I want and take a day off when I want!" This is all true. But I'm sure you can see the potential problems here.

Yes, you're free to choose when you work. Except if your goal is to make any money from your work, in which case, you'll quickly realise that you don't have as much of a choice as you thought. Whatever your chosen career, the rule (at least at the beginning) is simply: if you don't work, you don't earn. And sadly, there is no corollary that if you work you earn, meaning it's entirely possible to work and not earn!

If your long-term goal is to set up a huge e-commerce or online marketing business that one day will generate passive income (income that's generated automatically without you having to do anything), you still have to set everything up, test it, maintain it and market it. It could take months or even years before you see the fruits of your labour churning out enough cash to live on.

3. **Overwhelm,** Deciding what to do and in which order can be completely daunting. There is *so much* to think about when you HomeWork: planning your time, prioritising projects, sticking to your routine, analysing your progress towards your goals, staying productive and motivated. It's very easy to feel like you don't know where to start. If you feel overwhelmed in this way, breathing is your friend. Friends are also your friend. When you don't have colleagues to bounce ideas off, talking things out with friends and family can really help you sort through your thoughts. Sometimes, just saying what the problem is out loud will help you see the solution. Then get your planner out, prioritise a few things to do, and get going.

So you see, it's actually not easy. But the idea is that eventually, you'll get used to being the boss!

The Employee

It's helpful to remember that at home, you are your own employee. Even remote workers who have a structured hierarchy back at the office need to think this way to a degree when HomeWorking. How well you inhabit this role determines how effective your HomeWork will be.

To elucidate this further, a thought experiment: perhaps you've been someone else's boss before, perhaps not. Either way, try to imagine that you own and operate a small business (or a big one, if you prefer to be a Big Dog in your own thought experiments!). Now, imagine that you have a team of employees who work for you. You must now consider all of the following things related to your employees: how long and how hard they work, how the expectations and work conditions you place upon them affect their wellbeing, how that, in turn, affects their productivity and longevity at the company, and how all of it affects your bottom line and profits.

It may sound obvious, but it's worth noting that every single one of these issues still applies to you as a HomeWorker. The better you can get at being a good employee, the better your business will do, and the happier your boss (you) will be!

How to Be a Good Boss and a Good Employee

Let's think about ways in which you can inhabit these two roles concurrently and effectively. Try to embody the qualities you want from a boss. Try to work like you'd want your own employees to work.

A Good Boss:

- **Is decisive, and owns their decisions.** Make a choice, take responsibility for it, implement it.

- **Is a clear communicator.** Sort your thoughts out on paper, organise them into an action plan, make priorities, set clear goals and parameters for each project.

- **Understands their employees' needs.** Don't expect miracles from yourself. Be aware of the demands you place on your time, the pressure you put on yourself, the hours you work.

A Good Employee:

• **Works diligently and meets the targets set for them.** Make sure you're tracking your progress and meeting your own targets. If you're falling short, ask yourself whether it's the fault of Boss-you, for setting unrealistic targets, or Employee-you for not managing your time efficiently.

• **Is professional.** Even if you work alone, professionalism is vital. In your work, your correspondence, your attitude, your mindset. If you don't think and act like a professional, how do you expect anyone to treat you like one?

• **Challenges the status quo.** Questioning the wisdom of the path you're treading is a good idea. And you don't have to worry about aggravating the boss by piping up. Always be prepared to re-think your decisions if they're not leading you where you want to go.

• **Shows up for work.** I mean this both physically and mentally. So keep to a set working schedule each day and don't "leave work" until you're done.

MiniWin: Set Your Expectations

Write a list with two columns. One for what you expect from yourself as a boss, the other as an employee. Boil it down to short phrases like "I will make decisions and stick to them," or "I will be on time to work every day," or "I want more breaks."

As a Boss...	As an Employee...
E.g. I'll give my employee positive feedback.	*E.g. I'll commit to finishing projects on time.*

When you have a clearer picture of what your Boss-self and your Employee-self want and need, you'll be able to plan your HomeWorking day better. Stick the list up somewhere you can see it every day, and now you know what you expect of yourself, let's think about ways of getting the most out of your workday.

How to Maximise Your Work Day - Even if You Only Have Limited Working Hours

There are countless ways to handle your time and task management. If you've not tried following a specific method beyond "having a to do list", then my advice is to head back over to Google or YouTube, where you'll find countless different methods and approaches. Try as many of them as you can to figure out what works best for you over time. Some will suit your natural rhythms and tendencies better than others.

Naturally, everyone is bound by how much they can get done in the time they have, and if you're really only able to work part-time, then you'll need to adjust your expectations especially if you've previously been used to 9-5, Monday to Friday. But over the years, I've found ways of maximising my workday.

I used to have all the time in the world. It felt like it anyway. Then I had kids! But here's the funny thing — and I know other HomeWorking parents out there feel this way too — having less available work time has the effect of focussing you and actually *increases* your productivity. I can get way more done in 4-6 hours now than I could in 8-10 in my twenties. Back then, I knew I had ample time to finish things, so things naturally got left until the last minute!

I think it's not just a "having kids" phenomenon, though, it's age too. As we age, we literally have less time left on Earth, which does tend to focus one's mind somewhat on getting your goals ticked off!

All that said, it's been a long, grinding struggle to get to a place where I know I can cram a lot into a day and not get too frazzled. I'd say it's been the greatest struggle of my HomeWorking career, and now that I've mastered it, it's a source of great pride.

Now, everyone will have things that work best for them. You may like planning with Post-it notes, you may prefer a paper planner, or a whiteboard. You may use planning software, or perhaps like me, you use all of these in combination? The point is, you *must* have a plan. You can curate it, change it, develop it, even throw it out and start again, but you *must* have a plan, and use it as the basis for setting tasks for the day / week / month ahead.

Adopt the ADOPTED Planning Method

After many years of trial and error, trying different software, products, techniques and methods to stay organised, this is the best productivity process I've come up with.

A.D.O.P.T.E.D

Analyse > Decide > Organise > Plan > Test > Execute > Discipline

Analyse >

This is the free-thinking, blue sky, beginning of your journey on each project. What is it you want to do? Whether it's a big question like, "What do I want to do with my life?" or a relatively straightforward one like, "What's the best way to grow my online audience?" before you can answer, you'll need to make sure you've looked at the question from all angles, researched possible strategies, and found out what impact those approaches will have on you and your career. This is where you stress-test ideas. Read books, do online courses, find helpful resources, seek advice, watch YouTube videos about your subject. Be thorough, but beware…

> ***"Analysis Paralysis"****, where you endlessly contemplate ideas without actually getting started on anything. It's impossible to know whether you're onto a winning strategy until you try it for a while. Research is crucial, yes, but just don't get stuck researching and never actually producing anything.*

It's easy to get fired-up about ideas and projects, and to think ahead to what their conclusion would look like for you and your business. But then you realise that the only person who can make that idea come to fruition is you. I struggle with this one, and have had to design ways to handle it.

If you're like me, you have a dozen or so "killer ideas" a week. They're not all killers, obviously, but they always feel like it at the time! That's why it's important to have a triage system to capture and store them, then put them through analysis before deciding whether or not to action them.

I have a large ideas folder with plans for novels, screenplays, albums and businesses. At least five to ten ideas for every one I've eventually completed. Every new idea needs testing. Ask yourself questions like "Will this idea benefit my chosen goals *directly*? How long will it take to complete? How long before it has an impact? What other paths might it lead me down (and do I *want* to go down them?) Is there a market for what I've come up with? Will I be able to remain motivated if I pursue this idea? *Will I finish it*?"

Having asked all these questions of yourself, if you still don't have a concrete answer, that's your answer. If it was a goer, you'd know by now. File it away in your ideas folder, maybe bring it out again for an airing at a later date, but don't get stuck in analysis paralysis, move on to the next idea.

If, however, you feel good about pursuing the idea, move on to the next step.

> Decide >

Possibly the most important step, and often the hardest. The analysis phase is over, it's time to make a decision and stick to it (at least for now). This means committing to the new project and including it in your schedule.

> Optimise >

This is where you organise your thoughts and make sure that what you're about to take on is both realistically achievable in the time you have, and likely to contribute to your overall progress towards your goals, whatever they are. If the answer to either of these is no, go back to the analysis stage.

If you're happy to proceed, write down your goal, your approach, and the tasks you're going to need to do in order to get it done. Break the whole thing down.

This is also the phase where you can invest some time in learning to teach yourself about what you're about to do. Are you going to need to learn any new skills? Will it require the use of a new piece of software? Do you need to invest any money upfront? Is there any training you could look at that would help you get this project off the ground?The learning you do here will inform the planning stage.

> Plan >

Planning your tasks efficiently is make-or-break for the HomeWorker. There are lots of tips and hacks to planning, which we'll go into later. Whatever planning regimen you end up using, get a plan down on paper/screen/planner/whiteboard. Make sure it fits around your working days and, as mentioned before, that it's realistically achievable.

Choose a timeframe for the project — you could even give yourself a deadline, though bear in mind that as you progress through it, you'll discover new things that may either lengthen or shorten your expected completion date. The better-organised your early planning has been, the more adaptable you'll be as the project develops.

> Test >

Before you begin each task within your project, it's important to define and state what its completion will look like.

"Completion Depletion". *At the opposite end of the spectrum from "analysis paralysis" is not being able to finish things. I've searched for a term for this but found none, so I came up with "Completion Depletion": the lack of complete tasks and projects. As the list of unfinished tasks grows, so you become more and more depleted, both in terms of your physical, measurable progress, but also when it comes to your reserves of self-belief and sense of worth. If getting stuff done makes you feel good, "completion depletion" can have a terrible impact on your self-confidence and motivation.*

So, once you've broken down, prioritised and ordered your tasks, set up a completion test for each one by giving it a **measurable outcome**. For example, if you're writing a book, make your task something like "write Chapter 3 conclusion," or "sort out formatting for Kindle Direct," both of which are better than having a goal to write a specific word count, say. If you're designing a website, tasks like "Add contact form to sidebar," and "Resize logo for mobile site," are better than "finish homepage". You get the idea.

Tip: overestimate the time you allocate to each task. See the MiniWin below!

> Execute >

You heard what Shia LaBeouf said: do it! (Or, if you prefer, Ben Stiller in *Starsky & Hutch*). It's time to get going with the work. If you've planned properly, this should be a fairly straightforward process of completing the various tasks in the order you've set and testing their completion against the stated outcome you came up with in the **Test** stage, before ticking them off and moving on. If you don't find that it's working out this way and you get stuck, or find yourself moving on to work on something else, you've probably not thought the project through clearly yet: go back and re-do your planning stage.

> Discipline >

This is how you keep the train on the rails. The only way of moving through your plan and getting done the things you know you need to, is to develop and maintain discipline. Keep your momentum up. The scientific phrase often applied here comes from Newton's first law of motion: an object in motion stays in motion, and an object at rest stays at rest. Try to always be the former, not the latter!

Ultimately, how hard — or more accurately, how *efficiently* — you work will depend on your ability to move through each of the ADOPTED stages in a methodical and disciplined way. If you're the kind of person who finds following through on ideas difficult because you keep having new ones (I often fall into this category), then taking this step by step approach and holding yourself accountable along the way makes it a lot easier to reach the finish line for each task and, therefore, the entire project.

Similarly, if you just like to get your head down and get on with things but sometimes lack the structure or direction of a well-thought-out plan, keeping yourself to the Optimise, Plan and Test methodology will help you to define and measure progress towards a goal, which will stop you wasting time doing "busy work" and instead, focus your efforts on working shrewdly.

Don't Let Interruptions Interrupt

It's a definite downside of HomeWorking that there are things that will happen at home that are unrelated to your work and will seek to distract you from it.

If you're the only one home, for example, you're always potentially "on-call" as the Representative of the Dwelling. Dealing with deliveries, tradespeople, appointments, unexpected visits and errands can be a major productivity-killer.

Some of these distractions are within your control. Putting a sign up on the door that asks delivery drivers to leave packages in a safe place will hopefully prevent them from ringing the doorbell, unless they need a signature. Obviously, you want to refrain from booking appointments, or having people scheduled to come round during your work hours if an alternative time is possible.

Do your level best to keep those distractions that are beyond your control from knocking you off course. There's not much you can do if the doorbell rings. But after you've politely accepted your delivery, don't open it! Unless it's directly related to the task you're currently working on, of course. Keep your mind where it was when the doorbell went, put the package down to look at later and get straight back to work.

If your phone rings, you'll have to judge whether or not you need to speak to that person *right now*. Yes, it might be someone calling with an emergency. Make your friends and family aware of what hours you keep and ask them nicely to respect that, keeping calls outside that time. Then, if one of them does call during work hours, it's likely to be more important, and you should take the call. If someone can't get through to you the first time and desperately needs to, they'll call back, text, try your email, your Facebook. Chances are, most calls you receive can actually wait until you're ready to speak.

Otherwise, call friends back when your work is done. Use your common sense. You know that if you speak to a friend, the likelihood is that you'll end up having a long chat. That's why they're your friend, you get along! Try not to indulge in this kind of call, pleasurable as they are, during your precious work time. Save it up for break time or the end of the day.

Manage Your Notifications

In a similar vein to triaging your phone calls, you'll need to have a disciplined approach to how you react to notifications. Be it email, social media post alerts, your news feed, a new podcast upload, a new WhatsApp message…the list goes on. When a notification goes off, the temptation is to immediately check it out, which as we all know, can be a major distraction. It's possible to get "shiny object syndrome" and chase after the notification in case it leads to something important, fun or rewarding.

In his book *Indistractable,* Nir Eyal refers to these "pings, dings and rings" as "external triggers" for distraction. He asks whether they serve us, or if we end up serving them.

Having your notifications on means that you're essentially saying to yourself: "I'm OK being distracted from the tasks I set myself." Think about it: you've set some time aside for your next task. You've decided that it's worth doing. But you haven't set time aside to deal with an email that comes in, or check your feeds, or get on WhatsApp to enjoy some banter with your friends. It only takes one distraction to knock you off course and potentially eat up time that would otherwise have been spent on the task at hand. If the task is worth doing, ignore the notifications. Or better still: switch them off completely, even if it's temporarily until you complete your task.

Have set times of day devoted to checking your social media, the news, your messages and handling email. Don't allow yourself to look at them at other times. With no distracting notifications, this becomes much easier.

As I wrote this very section, an email ping went off. I saw the subject of the email but managed not to click on it, and saved it for later. I returned immediately to writing this. I've now followed my own advice and switched off email notifications while writing! On macOS, it's in System Preferences > Notifications > Mail. You can set them to None, Banners or Alerts, and toggle several other settings. To get the sound to stop you have to go into Mail > Preferences > General and set New Messages Sound to "none".

Errands

We all sometimes need to pay a visit to someone or to get something done. As hard as it may be to schedule these things around your work life, do try to respect the sanctity of your working day if you can. Plan ahead to accommodate the interruption to your working week. If you have to make that doctor's appointment, or you have to pick up your dry cleaning today, consider working early or late to make up for the time you lose.

Make Your Workspace Desirable

Some people are very visual and really do find that what they look at throughout the day can affect their mood, productivity or creativity.

If you're someone who derives motivation from visual stimuli, you need to make sure you recognise this need in the design of your workspace. It doesn't need to be anything fancy or expensive.

Include things like paintings, posters, objets d'art, inspiring quotes, photos of your family and pets…all things to keep you motivated throughout the day.

Consider how comfortable and *desirable* your workspace is. I don't just mean how ergonomic your chair is — though having your chair/desk/screen/keyboard/mouse set up in correct ergonomic relation is, of course, vital. What I want you to ask yourself is, how much do I *want* to spend time here?

Even if your workspace is the corner of a room that has another purpose entirely — like a bedroom or living room — your little corner should be somewhere that you want to be. Once you've made it look good, you need to make it *feel* good.

Things to think about:

Music/Radio. Many people love a little background noise while they work. I can't think of anything worse, personally…even the wonderful sound of birds chirping outside my garden studio sometimes irks me! Maybe it's the musician in me, meaning I'm more likely to 'tune in' to what I hear and start analysing it. I like working in silence.

But there are studies that show a degree of low-level noise can boost your focus and productivity, so if you're someone who's not bothered by it, consider tuning your radio to some nice music (classical works best according to the scientists) or a talk show hosted by a presenter with a nice, mellifluous voice.

Natural Light. This is a must. Not only does it affect your mood (which, as we all know, can affect your work), but it also influences your body clock. Whether you're an Early Bird or a Night Owl, keeping to a regular daily routine is much easier if you make sure to keep your body's internal time (known as your circadian rhythm) attuned to nature's rhythm. In other words, make sure you see daylight while it's available!

This could be tricky if you work in a space with no windows, such as a basement. If this is the case, try to build in enough time away from your desk to get some exposure to natural light, like going for a walk at lunchtime or taking a break in the garden.

Those who suffer from Seasonal Affective Disorder (SAD) know that they need to get enough exposure to daylight, or their bodies can produce too much melatonin (making them sleepy) and serotonin (affecting their general mood, sleep and appetite). You need to get daylight directly on your eyeballs regularly for best results (this means going outside or opening a window, it doesn't work as well through glass). The vitamin D you get from exposure to sunlight is also important for health.

Whether you suffer from SAD or not, we can all benefit from getting proper daylight, so try to get plenty into your workspace if you can, since you'll be spending a long time there every day.

And obviously, if you're outside in sunny weather, remember to listen to Baz Luhrmann and use sunscreen.

Artificial Light. Though not as beneficial to health as natural light, this can improve the ambience and aesthetics of your workspace, especially as the light outside changes. I have many different sources of light in my studio, including overhead Halogen bulbs, a giant Pixar-style angle-poise floor lamp illuminating my desktop, a colour-changing remote controlled lamp that sits on the floor pointing up at the wall (this is great for conjuring different moods at different times of day) and various other light sources around the place.

Having the ability to mix and match your lighting allows you to control the ambience in your workspace, and it also has a practical purpose. For example, when I'm writing music by hand, I need good illumination, so I'll switch my Pixar lamp on. However, if you're going to be looking at the computer monitor for a long time, especially at night, it's important to keep lighting levels low. Gently illuminating the wall behind your monitor — a technique called bias lighting — reduces eye strain (because science). Additionally, most new monitors have a setting that reacts to ambient light, darkening when the room dims. This assists with your circadian rhythm because looking at a bright screen right before bed has been shown to hamper your ability to get to sleep.

Comfort. The more comfortable you are, the better you're going to be able to concentrate for longer periods. We've talked about the importance of ergonomics, but there are other considerations when thinking about your comfort. And you'll *want* to spend time in your workspace, too. Think about cushions, footrests, having a different place to sit than your desk chair (I have a sofa in the studio, which is good for reading on).

Clothing. This is linked to comfort. Now, you might say, "but my PJs are my most comfortable clothing!" But we talked about that earlier. Have clothes that you specifically wear during the day, and choose comfortable ones. You don't have to look fancy, but ask yourself if you'd be happy to be seen in what you're wearing if the doorbell rings, or if you have a video call with a client!

> *Sartorial side note: it's often joked about — at least among my friendship group — HomeWorkers can work in our underpants. I have to say that, whilst most days I can be found wearing jeans and a shirt, there have been some hot summers where the only feasible item of clothing was the underpant, or swimming shorts! My studio gear gives off tremendous heat, and in spaces without air conditioning, it can heat the room to a fierce temperature. I always keep some clothes nearby to throw on in case the door goes, naturally. So yes, sometimes, I have worked in my underpants. Don't judge me. I'm just trying to be comfortable and maximise productivity. I bet some of you do it too…*

Things to Avoid Whilst Working

TV

As we learned above, science says working with the radio playing quietly is OK. However this doesn't go for the TV; it's just too distracting. The visual element means there will always be something pulling your focus. Unless you sit where you can't see the screen, I guess. But then you may as well just have the radio on!

There is a third way, of course: use your computer itself. Type "music to study to" into YouTube. You're welcome!

Cooking Meals

The day to day necessities of life can get in the way of your work, like making food and drinks, for example! Try not to spend your precious work hours preparing meals. That's what weekends and evenings are for. Make lunch as quick to prepare as breakfast. If it's not, plan ahead and prep while you're sorting breakfast, or the night before. For me, breakfast is usually a smoothie, and if I have lunch, it's something I can grab from the fridge and throw on a plate, either leftovers from last night or a salad.

Have easy access to food and drink. Keep your fridge and cupboards well-stocked. If you're a snacker, have your snacks to hand. You don't need to get to lunchtime and then realise you'll have to go out to the shops to get some food. If you're a caffeine junkie, put your coffee making facilities nearby. I keep an espresso machine in my home office, which saves me from me having to go back over to the house to use the one in the kitchen, which would disrupt the flow of my work. Given my love of the bean, that would add up over the course of the week to a lot of time away from my desk!

See Chapter 7: HomeWorker Diet *for a deeper dive into your role as Head of Catering!*

Mail

Don't open your mail while working. As we discussed before, it's likely to distract you, or provide you with a new 'to do' for your list, either business or personal. If it's a package of something you've ordered, you could be in danger of losing the afternoon to playing with your new toy! Even if it is business-related — and the likelihood in this day and age is, very little mail will be — it almost certainly won't be related to the task you're currently on. Mail can almost always wait until you're "off the clock".

Email

This is a tricky one if your business requires you to email (are there businesses that *don't?*). So I suggest you block out time to deal with your inbox and stick to only dealing with it in those periods, even if you see new ones coming in through the day. Once you've moved on to other tasks, shut down your email app. I'd recommend diarising one main email session per day, and perhaps one small check-in later on for triage.

YOUR INBOX IS A LIST OF OTHER PEOPLE'S AGENDAS...JUST BECAUSE YOU'VE CLEARED YOUR INBOX, IT DOESN'T MEAN YOU'VE ACCOMPLISHED ANYTHING.

Tim Ferriss

Social Media

Again, if your business model includes using social media, you're going to have to work out strict boundaries for yourself in terms of the time and scope of your use. Setting up a Facebook ad campaign for your business is one thing, but then spending twenty minutes after that checking your feed is a no-no. Save it for your downtime (and maybe also skip it then and have some *real* downtime!).

Sleep: Are You a Night Owl, or an Early Bird?

There is probably a time of day (or night) when you feel you're at your most productive. Whether this is at the crack of dawn, mid-morning or late at night, this is the part of your day when you can reliably smash through your to-do list. It's worth finding out which you are so you can load the most taxing or creative tasks into that time period each day.

We all have different "chronotypes", meaning we exhibit behaviours dictated by our individual circadian rhythms, such as when we prefer to go to sleep. In general (though not exclusively), we tend to be night owls when we're young, and, as we get older, we switch to being early birds. This won't be true for everyone, but it certainly was for me. I used to love the calm of night time and the feeling that I had the world to myself while everyone else slept. But that was when I could sleep in late! As soon as you have kids, you're going to be waking up when they do, so staying awake working into the wee small hours becomes unfeasible. That's what precipitated the switch for me.

And it turns out that, if you get up early enough, you can still experience the feeling of calm solitude that night owls enjoy. I was once eulogising about the joys of waking early to my wife, who keeps "regular" office hours, works incredibly hard, and is one of those people who could happily sleep for twelve hours a night if circumstance permitted. When I said how much I loved feeling like I had the world to myself at 5 am, she insouciantly commented: "That's fine, you can have it…I'll be happily sleeping." It made me chuckle, and reminded me that we all have our own rhythms that work best!

Getting Up Early

More and more people are trying the early bird thing these days. I haven't read Hal Elrod's *The Miracle Morning* or Robin Sharma's *The 5am Club*, but the chances are I've been influenced by the movement that these two books and many like them have brought about in recent years. In the spirit of life-hacking and productivity-boosting that's become so popular lately, people are trying out waking up super early.

For me, I first tried it a couple of years ago as a way to alleviate the time pressures I was feeling during the working day. I need to fit my work around the kids' school hours, which effectively shortens the workday to around 5-6 hours (9am to 3pm). Even less if you want to exercise during that time! I wanted time back during the day, and I was willing to try anything to get it.

The very first time I tried it, I became a convert. I set the alarm for 5 am, crept downstairs and set to work. It was beautifully peaceful in the house. The kids wake between 6 and 7, so I had at least an hour to myself. I discovered something: my brain works well at that time! I was able to focus and work hard, do deep thinking, be creative. Once the coffee kicked in, of course.

THE MUSES LOVE THE MORNING.

Thomas Fuller

The best part of it was how I felt once everyone else was 'up and running' with their day, and the usual pre-school chaos of breakfast, getting dressed and getting out the door for the school run had started. Not only was I, by now, full energised — and therefore able to handle the kids with more patience and playfulness than if I'd just rolled out of bed and was groggy — but crucially I had the feeling of having already banked a couple of hours of work in the day, o having achieved something! I can't tell you how much this feeling has affected my overall wellbeing and happiness.

So then when I return from the school run, and it's not even 9 yet, I don't feel quite so guilty about going out for a run. Before I was waking early, I felt I needed to get straight to work. Not so anymore, and fitting in the run at 9 to re-energise me for the second work session of the day works for me.

Try it! I heartily recommend seeing whether it works for you, because if it does, it's a great way of squeezing more time out of the day (and hence your life). The trade-off is that you'll need to go to bed earlier. But I realised when I switched to this routine that I'd rather watch fewer Netflix episodes per night than be constantly under pressure during my work hours. I still get a good couple of hours after the kids go to bed to hang out with my wife and unwind at the end of the day. But now I go to bed between 9 and 10 instead of between 11 and 12.

> *Note: I have found that this schedule works best in combination with a low or no-carb diet. When I was eating carbs, I had some powerful post-lunch energy lulls and couldn't keep my eyes open! It would negate the point of waking early if I needed an afternoon nap to accommodate it. But cutting the carbs meant that this stopped happening, and I could work through.*

Another benefit is that you'll not be in danger of snacking a few hours after dinner when hunger strikes: because you'll already be asleep by then!

It may take some time for your body to adjust, but it will.

Here are some tips to make getting up early work best:

• If you have one available, consider sleeping in a separate bed from your partner on nights when you intend to wake early. If they're not getting up at the same time as you, you risk disrupting their sleep. If you are going to sleep in the same bed, make sure your alarm is a nice gentle one. I like "Slow Rise" on the iPhone.

• Don't snooze. I'll say it again: do not snooze! Snoozing achieves nothing; you'll remain sleepy and tired until you get up and get going. It's been proven that snoozing sleep is not restful, restorative sleep. It may, in fact, be bad for our health. Once your REM sleep has been interrupted by your alarm, your fight or flight response is triggered, and your blood pressure and heartbeat increase (which it's supposed to, having dropped while you sleep). A few minutes until the alarm goes off again is not long enough to put your body back into restorative sleep mode, so all you're doing is holding yourself in a limbo state and missing out on the time that you set your alarm in order to gain! So, if you're *not* one of those annoying people like me who can just leap straight out of bed when the alarm goes off, you're going to have to commit to digging deep and just getting out of bed in order to make this work. Come on, up and at 'em, the day's a-wastin'!

• Get straight to work. OK, you can make a quick coffee first if you need to, but don't start your day reading your newsfeed or checking social media. You've set your alarm for a reason, so make the most of it. Make sure you know what your first task of the day is the night before so that when you sit down at your computer, you can set to it. I tend to write, so the first thing I do is fire up Pages. I've learnt to bypass Safari and Mail!

• Don't look at your phone, for the same reason as above. There's nothing there that will help you get your work done! Save it for a break later on.

• Make sure the kids know that this is your work time, since they may wake up long before they need to start getting ready for school. Mine happily watch some TV during this time, and we've usually left them some fruit and a water bottle out the night before, so I don't have to run around after them right away. 7 is usually the cut off when I stop working, gather the kids up, and the three of us go and wake Mummy up with cuddles in bed before we start getting ready.

• You know how much sleep you need. This is only going to work for you long-term if you make sure you get it, and that means committing to the earlier night. It's not like you'll miss anything in this age of streaming and catch-up TV! If, however, you're simply not willing to give up some of your evening time to this end (or if you require a full 8-10 hours every night, otherwise you can't function), then early rising is not for you.

• Relax the rules at weekends. I don't get up at 5 on Saturday or Sunday. I enjoy a 'sleep in' until 7 or 8 (I can hear my twenty-year-old self laughing hysterically at that sentence). I stay up later, and I allow myself carbs. I also tend not to exercise at weekends — spending time with the kids usually involves a significant degree of calorie-burning in any case! Naturally, I do go to bed early on Sunday night, ready for 5 am the next day.

> *Sartorial side note: Contrary to my advice earlier, during the period between 5 am and whenever you get washed and dressed, I would say that it* is *acceptable to work in your PJs. Full disclosure, I'm doing so right now! It would slow down your early morning start if you had to ablute and clothe yourself, not to mention the fact you could risk waking other members of your household. Better to just get on with it and get ready later. A cut-off point by which you should be out of your jammies and dressed for the day? I'd say 10 am. Beyond that, you're pushing it ;-)*

Procrastination & How to Deal With it

We all fall foul of the P-word from time to time. I certainly have, and doubtless will again. Those procrastination demons carry with them a tempting and seductive bounty of distracting activities, designed to stimulate your physical and mental receptors and dissuade you from getting on with your work, either by being so pleasurable in and of themselves, or by delivering their pleasure by dint of their contrast with the pain (or imagined pain) of working.

It *can* actually be rather beneficial to procrastinate (see number 7. below), and in small doses, it can add thread to the rich tapestry of life. But it's when the visits from those demons become too frequent, and the effect of your spending time with them becomes significantly deleterious to your work that you risk losing momentum, motivation and stalling your progress towards your goals.

Below are some perspectives and methods that will help you in your struggle against these wily demons with their clickbait videos, Facebook quizzes and messy sock drawers.

- **Don't start!** You've got a plan, you've got your time organised. Stick to it, and if you feel yourself beginning to procrastinate with something else, really try to say to yourself: "Just don't start this, carry on with the task at hand." It's by no means easy, but sometimes the best way to stop doing something is just not to start it. Of course, if you *don't* have a plan, then you won't necessarily know what the task at hand is supposed to *be,* meaning you'll be far more at risk of falling prey to the procrastination demons as you cast about for something to do.

- **Avoid boredom by mixing up tasks**. The longer you spend on one task, the more vulnerable you'll be to procrastinating. For example, if you plan to spend the entire day writing, you're likely to run out of steam at some point, and the temptation to do something else will increase. But if you plan an achievable and measurable amount of writing in, say 2,000 words or three hours, you'll have a target to aim for. Once finished, move onto a different task for a bit to keep your brain engaged.

- **Make your workspace less fun**. Get rid of anything that leads you to distraction. This could be a guitar leaning up against the wall, a Rubik's cube, a book, or the worst procrastination-enabler of them all, your phone! If you struggle with leaving the thing alone for more than five minutes, keep it in the other room while you work.

- **Distraction-proof your phone**. If you really must have your phone with you, switch off notifications and employ its "Do Not Disturb" mode so you can really focus. Sometimes, it will just take one ping to derail a train of thought or redirect your energies away from progress.

- **Move apps** that you use most off the home screen and replace them with more boring, useful, productive apps that won't hold your interest. We all know where the apps we use most regularly are on our home screens, and if you pick up your phone in a moment of distraction, and you're not careful, you'll find that your fingers automatically select your three or so most-used apps, sometimes without you consciously knowing it. So move them — out of sight, out of mind. You could even tuck them away inside a folder and call it: "Are you sure?" or "Time Wasters"!

- **Make a B-list.** Sometimes, despite your best efforts, you just won't be "feeling" the task you're on. No matter how important it is to your plans, sometimes your brain will just be in another place entirely. But that doesn't mean you have to fall foul of procrastination. Have a B-list of tasks ready for these times:

a "break glass in case of loss of focus". B-list tasks are less urgent than your A-list (AKA your to-do list), and should be more fun or engaging, but they should also be things that, however loosely, count as work. They can scratch the itch of procrastination without taking you out of your work headspace, or making you feel guilty.

Examples of B tasks include:

• *Watch a YouTube video.* Build up a back catalogue in your "Watch Later" list of tutorials and other work-related content.

• *Tidy up.* If your workspace has grown cluttered and messy, stick a podcast or some music on and enjoy some tidy up time! Note: don't allow this to spiral into full-on housework, limit it to your workspace *only*!

• *Go on social media.* You heard me! Find a comfy spot, take a short "break" and go on Instagram, Facebook, Twitter, Pinterest. But not to look at deep fakes, memes, cats or celebs…this is still "work time", so make sure you're keeping it to promotion or building up your followers.

• *Delve into your "someday" file.* You've had some big ideas that have struck you over the years as eureka moments, and you've written them down, then never gotten around to actioning them. I have a folder called "Ideas", which is heaving with potential projects, none of which have made it onto my A-list, but all of which have fired my imagination at some point. Take some time to swim inside these ideas again. Follow up on one, even if it's just to expand your notes. You never know, it might become an A-list idea!

Think of B-list tasks as palette-cleansers. Limit your time on B-tasks to 10-20 minutes, then get back to your A-list refreshed, or with a new idea.

- **Take a break.** Just reset your brain with some rest…it's easy to overwork yourself when there's no one around to invite you to the break room or out to lunch! Remember: whatever it takes…apply the brakes!

- And finally…**don't deal with it!** On occasion, you don't have to stop yourself from procrastinating. Sometimes, it's a good thing to let your brain slide into a different gear for a while. And it's healthy to treat yourself. So if you feel you've been working hard, and you haven't let the demons in for a while, have at it. **Just don't make a habit of it!**

White Space

This trendy term refers to the need for us to program some space just to think into our schedule. More than that, it's space to *deep think*. To contemplate, meditate, consider, even just to let your mind wander. Studies have shown that some of the best ideas come out of this state of mind (remember the old adage about getting ideas when you're in the bathroom? White space! I wonder if that's why most toilets are white?).

Some companies have begun to buy into this, and rather than making their employees run around from meeting to meeting, and allowing them to cram their planners full of overlapping, impossible-to-complete-in-the-time-they-have-tasks, they are asking their workers to plan in timed white space every day.

This particularly helps those of us who are creative. Anyone who needs to access that part of their brain for their job will tell you that sometimes, it's nigh on impossible to find the inspiration to have a good idea, to express yourself truthfully, or to "make good art", as Neil Gaiman puts it. White space allows us the time and mental clarity to enter this zen state of mind, where the alpha waves are flowing and the ideas run freely.

Alpha waves are the brainwaves that occur when we're in this "flow state" of energised yet calm focus. They are the subject of many studies into mindfulness and stress reduction. Getting yourself into this mental state comes with all kinds of physiological and mood-altering benefits too.

You're your own boss, remember, so no one's going to plan this stuff into your day for you. You have to be bold, get over the guilt you may feel about "not working" (because it is working, just in a different way), and put some time for white space into your daily planner. Just 10 minutes is sometimes enough.

How to Use White Space

Find a quiet place (it's best if it's different from the spot you work at, but remember not to let your HomeWorker life spill over into your home life — so don't get into bed or anything!). If there's nowhere at home, go and sit in the car, find a nice spot in the garden, the park, or anywhere you won't be distracted.

Then, as you would if you were beginning a meditation, let every thought that's buzzing around your head slip away. If it comes back, that's OK, don't let it stress you out, just concentrate on letting it move to the side. It will all still be there when you're done. Now...zoom out. Zoom out of your head, of your place (picture yourself in one of those Google Earth camera zoom-outs, if it helps) and see everything.

Think *perspective*, an important word, which we'll return to later.

Breathe. See beyond this day, this week, what's on, who's where, what you have to finish, and when. Think beyond yourself.

And then...let those alpha waves roll, baby! Your blood pressure will reduce, your heart rate will slow, your concentration and focus will be honed, your sense of wellbeing will increase, and your creativity will begin to manifest. Not surprising then, that having spent time in this wonderful state, you'll likely have some very good ideas to put into practice; ideas that would not have come to the fore had you just kept busy-working.

When Not to Use White Space

However, a word of caution: white space can be a great tool, but it can also be used as an excuse to just not work. How many of you, especially the creative types, have had the experience of "just not feeling it" and, therefore, giving up and either starting a different task, or taking a break for some YouTube video-bingeing? After many years of procrastinating like this and learning strategies to overcome it, I learned that waiting "for the muse to descend" is really just an excuse not to create.

THE MUSE VISITS DURING THE PROCESS OF CREATION, NOT BEFORE. DON'T WAIT FOR HER. START ALONE.

Roger Ebert

OK, so you're not currently alive with your best ideas, but you don't just give up at the first hurdle. Each field of work will have its own examples of this, but as a composer, when I have a piece of music to write, and I'm feeling particularly uninspired, these are the strategies I try *before* I give myself some white space, especially if I'm on a deadline!

1. **Play**. I'll sometimes play around on the piano, improvising until something comes up that I like the sound of (again, I have to be careful to keep it purposeful and not to let it turn into a mammoth jam for pleasure!). This approach could be used with some free-form writing, writing in a journal, or doodling. Like stretching before a workout, it gets you using your creative muscles and allows the creative juices to flow.
2. **Commit**. Just get started. Put any idea down. Don't analyse it, just write it down. Then another, then another. Then try the first idea with the second, with the third, try the second and third together. See if anything comes of it. Repeat. Yes, this way of creating is more arbitrary and tedious than when it "just comes to you", but I always think "Hey, it's my job, sometimes it's hard work, get on with it." You can begin finessing once you have enough material to work with.
3. **Reframe**. Focus on a different element of the problem from the one that's troubling you. If I've been struggling to come up with a melody or a chord sequence, I'll switch focus to something else, like programming some percussion (if the track requires it), and that will take my mind off the melody and chords. The rhythms I come up with might then suggest accompaniment or melodic ideas and I can return to the original problem with new ideas.

Taking some time for white space (or knowing when not to and instead using the three methods above) is a great way to combat any barriers that are hampering your progress, like writer's block, analysis paralysis, problem-solving, planning, even feelings of overwhelm. And like meditation, it requires practice and discipline, but once you become adept at sliding into this mental state, it can yield some fantastic results. Give it a try!

Overestimate

A quick tip to make your daily schedule work well for you is to **always overestimate how long tasks will take you.** Then, if they do end up taking that long (or longer), you'll have lessened the feeling of guilt that accompanies not sticking to your schedule, not to mention you won't fall so behind on other tasks.

But, if you finish early, the positive thing is that you'll **create time**! Who doesn't wish they had more time? When you complete a task in 40 minutes that you'd set aside an hour for, not only will it feel like a win, but you'll also have created twenty minutes of freedom in which you can take a break, get started on the next task, read a book, go for a walk…you get the idea.

Be careful, though: Parkinson's Law says that **work will expand into the time allocated to it**. If you find this happening to you, it could mean a) you've *underestimated* the time and b) you haven't broken down the task into achievable chunks. Try fixing these two things in your planning.

Don't Grip it Too Tight

Let's be honest, we all struggle with productivity sometimes. Some days you just don't get as much done, or you feel a bit "meh", or life gets in the way. Any number of things can trigger the thought: "I haven't been as productive today as I wanted to be". Especially if the day before, you were a raging, alpha wave-surfing, ass-kicking ball of goal-smashing, getting-stuff-done energy.

But the truth is, this happens to us all, and may even be healthy. Losing momentum once in a while is normal. As long as you can pick it back up again the next day, don't be too hard on yourself. If you are struggling to keep your motivation going long-term, it could be worth checking in with your mental health and see if there are any underlying causes to your lack of productivity like excessive stress, anxiety or depression. Or maybe you've grown lethargic due to lack of exercise? Think about your diet — are you simply the victim of a post-meal blood sugar crash? If any of these things ring a bell, you know what to do: fix the cause rather than the symptom.

But if you can see no particular reason why you're not being a productivity machine today, to you I say: don't grip it too tight — like the golfer whose swing suffers the more frustrated she becomes. The harder she swings and the tighter she grips, the worse her swing gets. Just relax, accept that today's not going to be the most killer day of your career, and start again tomorrow. If you still have some of the working day left to go, maybe focus on some of the less important, easier tasks in your planner, just to give you a quick win and make sure the day hasn't been a total bust (these are tasks from your B-list — see above). This doesn't happen to me very often, but when it does, that's usually when my studio gets a tidy!

Takeaways

- Plan your time efficiently, working around your body and brain's natural rhythms and following a system that works for you.
- Try out the ADOPTED productivity method.
- Try waking up earlier (and going to bed earlier!).
- Make your workspace desirable and comfortable.
- Beat procrastination by eliminating distractions and staying disciplined.
- Don't grip it too tight.

MiniWin: Try Something New

This week, try **onc** of these things every day:

- Get up at **5 am.**
- Plan out your tasks using the **ADOPTED method.**
- Set aside some time **white space.**

At the end of the week, write down your experience in your notebook, answering these questions:

1. What benefit did it bring you?
2. What challenges did you face?
3. Would you do it again?
4. How can you build this into your daily routine so that you stick to it going forward?

If you end up updating your daily routine to include one of these techniques, that's great. You can then try the other two over the next two weeks!

That leads us nicely from the subject of productivity to another crucial factor in making HomeWork work for you: your wellbeing. Productivity and wellbeing don't have to be mutually exclusive as long as you have the right strategies, learn to check in with yourself and keep balance. Read on…

6. HomeWorker Wellbeing

Nothing will put a dampener on your productivity faster than if you've got something on your mind, worse still if you're struggling with mental illness of any kind.

As a boss, you have to take responsibility for your employees' wellbeing, or the business will suffer. That's no different for HomeWorkers. As an employee, and as a human, you have to take responsibility for yourself, or your wellbeing and happiness will suffer.

Below are some pointers for how to remain aware of your mental health and general wellbeing.

> ***Disclaimer***: *I'm not a mental health professional. All advice is borne of personal experience and research. I have experienced some of the issues I describe below myself; others I have knowledge of through listening to the experiences of people in my life. My own symptoms were related to stress, which was related to my work/life balance, and improved once I took responsibility for myself and took steps to improve the situation, which included seeking help from others. I'm sharing my experience and advice for the benefit of others, and I hope it's helpful to you. But if*

you are worried in any way about your mental or physical health, you know what to do: see a medical professional!

The Importance of Self-Care

This cannot be overstated to anyone, in any job. Be you an office worker, factory worker, shop worker, teacher, medical professional, celebrity, politician, or HomeWorker — you have to look after yourself. The need to be aware of our mental wellbeing (and the physical and mental risks if we aren't) are now much more widely-known than they used to be. That's great, but there's still a long way to go before we as a species can say we've all mastered how to live, work, love, raise kids, stay healthy and maintain all of our relationships *whilst staying mentally well.*

For HomeWorkers, the challenges can be even greater. The strain we can feel, the pressure we put on ourselves, the isolation and lack of support, the sheer grind of having to self-motivate and remain disciplined can take a massive toll. If you're thinking about HomeWorking, or you already are, you need to be aware of this danger, and put into place some coping mechanisms to deal with it.

Mental Health

In some ways, it's easier to check in with your own mental health when you're at home. There's no co-worker to distract you with gossip on your break, so you're free to think about where your head's at. You can even do some deep breathing or meditation, and no one will look at you funny. The separation that an office job gives us is that we tend to be "on" while we're there, then "off" back at home. The tendency is to think, "I can get through the day here because I know I'll switch off when I get home."

But in other ways, it's harder. There's no concerned friend around to say, "Are you OK?" if they notice that you seem more stressed than usual. And isolation in and of itself has been scientifically proven to be unhealthy for us humans. We require interaction and a sense of community for maximum wellbeing. So, if you're spending lots of time alone, it's absolutely critical that you take responsibility for your own wellbeing, and put habits in place to encourage it.

Here are some considerations:

There's No HR

There's no one working to look out for your rights and wellbeing at your home. It's just you. So don't put yourself under too much pressure. Don't overwork. Imagine Head-of-HR-you constantly warning Boss-you that Employee-you would have grounds for litigation if your work begins to affect your mental health!

Stress

We all know it can be a killer. It isn't always a bad thing, though. It can, at the right times, be a wonderful motivator and productivity enhancer. The key is knowing which kind of stress you're feeling, how much of it, and whether it has started to take a toll on you.

Here are some signs that your stress levels may be too high and need addressing:

- You regularly feel overwhelmed, under pressure or fatigued by your work.
- You're having difficulty sleeping.
- Your brain is always whirring about things other than the task at hand.

- Your general health is suffering.
- You're over-eating or drinking too much.
- You have a shorter fuse than usual; you're snapping at your loved ones.

Depression

This is another dangerous condition that requires the help of a medical professional. Some markers that can suggest depression are:

- You're sleeping more than usual.
- You feel lethargic.
- You're unmotivated.
- You have trouble focussing.
- Your mood is continuously low.
- You find everyday activities harder than usual.
- You're over-eating or drinking to much.

Anxiety

Anxiety can be incredibly debilitating, too, and it can seem like there are more and more reasons to feel anxious in today's world. There's some overlap with the symptoms of depression, for example, trouble sleeping, irritability, loss of focus and general fatigue. A key difference is that people suffering from anxiety are sometimes more "antsy" or "keyed up". They worry about the future, whereas depressed people tend to accept that it will be negative. Of course, neither outlook is a desirable one to have.

Anxiety can bring about very distressing thoughts, physical symptoms similar to stress like adrenalin spikes, racing heartbeats and increased blood pressure. It can, in severe cases, trigger a panic or anxiety attack, where you can become convinced you're having a heart attack or some other mortal episode, feel sick or have difficulty breathing. When it gets to this stage, it's often as a result of a prolonged period of feeling anxious. The stress chemicals build up in your system over time and can lead to this kind of eruption.

The Knock-On

Society is increasingly more aware of how dangerous these mental conditions and others like them can be, and how deleterious to our physical health they are. They manifest in so many harmful ways, and are not necessarily exclusive of each other — it's entirely possible to be anxious, stressed and depressed all at once.

So it's absolutely vital that you're aware of these conditions and that you watch out for any signs that you may be experiencing them.

Being Aware of How You Are

This is easier said than done. But if you're someone who considers themselves to have a stiff upper lip and finds it difficult not to just "get on with the day", I'm going to suggest that you spend a minute, just one minute, when you first sit down to start work in the morning to just be aware of how you're doing. How much pressure do you feel under? Do you feel particularly stressed today? Is your breathing normal? Are you having any anxiety symptoms like chest pains, laboured breathing, difficulty catching breath, heavy heart beating?

First off, if the answer to any of these questions is "yes", then **seek the advice of a medical professional**.

Once you've established that your symptoms are not those of something like an imminent heart attack but are instead related to mental health issues like stress or anxiety, take some time to think about why that is. Talk to someone, a family member, your partner, a friend, a therapist, even the internet. We've learnt so much about mental health and the importance of self-care in the last couple of decades, but there's still a way to go. If you can accept that it's *your* responsibility to keep an eye on your mental health and to take action if you think there's a problem, then you'll be a much happier, healthier HomeWorker.

How to Handle it When Things Get a Bit Much

If you are experiencing any of the symptoms mentioned above, then try these tips to reduce your stress.

Short term ways to calm down:

- Take a break.
- Get a change of scene.
- Go for a walk.
- Breathe deeply and/or meditate.
- Call a friend or loved one for support.
- If things are buzzing around your head, write them down. Getting them onto paper and out of your head is often enough to quell anxious thoughts.

Long term:

- Exercise regularly.
- Maintain a healthy diet.
- Don't drink too much alcohol.
- Don't smoke.
- Consider visiting a therapist.
- Try an app like Calm or Headspace.

- Look at your daily planning — are you over-scheduling?

Perspective

I truly believe that this word can save humanity. As HomeWorkers, we're often cut off from others' perspectives — and our own can become skewed.

We all live inside our tiny bubble of existence, often forgetting that everyone has their own bubble and different experiences, backgrounds, motivations, loves and pain. We see anything and anyone who creates (or appears to create) disharmony in our lives as being In The Wrong. That's sometimes true; other times we need to look inside ourselves at our reaction to that person more than we do at the person.

This is where perspective comes in — your perspective of yourself, others, your life, your very existence. And you might consider others' perspectives too, though there's not much you can do to change them. But you can at least understand them, or failing that, you can apply any insight you gain in thinking about their perspectives to your own, and perhaps thereby cope better with life's demands.

Some problems are urgent and require immediate, focussed attention. Like a health scare, for example. Others are caused by wounds that run so deep they require years of attention and may never go away. But for the other 99% of issues you face every day, try this coping mechanism: just think ***perspective.***

We're all busy, we all have a million to-dos and demands on our time and goals and ambitions and dreams and fears and pressure and stress. When it starts to feel a bit too much, I find that taking a moment to remember that we're on a tiny rock in an endless universe helps me to find perspective on my everyday problems and challenges. I mean really, think about it. The likelihood is that when set against that backdrop, the details of your tiny, inconsequential life will begin to slip out of such sharp focus and blend into a wider picture, where they belong. The fabric of your existence is expansive, so don't get hung up on its individual stitches.

Think about a problem you're having. It could be an annoyance you feel at someone, a frustration that something hasn't happened, or has happened. It could be something that happened today, or something you're worried might happen in the future. Now think about the planet you're on and your place within in, think about the 7 billion other humans dealing with their own issues. Think about the fact that one day you'll be dead and gone, and how likely it is that this particular problem will be on your mind as you drift off into nothingness (or whatever you believe happens when we die). The chances are what seems like a Big Deal right now will fall away into insignificance soon enough, to be replaced by the other Big Deals of the Day. So it's probably not worth letting it worry you *quite* so much.

Now, doesn't that feel better? Perspective, see?

Perspective on Others

Another important one. Though one of the big plusses about HomeWorking is that you're less likely to have to deal with a nasty boss or a co-worker with annoying habits, you will still have to deal with other humans, either in your business or in your personal life.

The Stoics believed that all we can control are our own actions and thoughts. The actions and thoughts of other people are beyond our control, and so we should not spend time and effort being concerned with them.

There are many books out there on personality types and the psychology of character, if you'd like to delve deeper. But here's some cod-psychology directly out of my experience, informed only by my own opinion and designed only to offer perspectives on people that I've found useful, in the hope that it will help you.

If someone's wronged you, or is proving difficult to manage, remember to take a moment and think of what perspective on that person you can take. This might help you to cope with whatever negative impact they're having on you.

Narcissists

A pain to deal with, yes. But pity them because they're usually very insecure. Greet their boastfulness and self-centredness with peaceful, calm acceptance. They can't help it. So don't worry about it.

Bullies

If you experience physical or mental bullying, report it to the authorities. If you have someone like this in your life, try to remove them from it. Bullying bosses are, in fact, what leads some people to choose HomeWorking in the first place. If that's you, I commend you for taking the proactive step to remove toxic elements from your life and trying to build a more positive existence. If, for whatever reason, removing bullies from your life is not a feasible option, then try to understand that the reasons for their behaviour are usually always that they've experienced pain at some point in their life that has led them to make these choices in their behaviour. Pity them, avoid them. Unless they hurt you or someone else, then report them.

Angry People

Anger is one of the worst symptoms of the human condition. We all experience it. In fact, many of us have dealt with some form of anger issue that has negatively affected our lives. Stress, anxiety and fear all feed it, and it bubbles up dangerously, either seeping out slowly through passive-aggressive or negative behaviour, or building up over time and erupting.

If you're feeling angry, your productivity will take a nosedive. You won't be able to think straight when you're in such a heightened state. Try to calm down, breathe and relax. Think perspective.

If you encounter someone being angry and abusive towards you, especially if whatever has made them angry has very little to do with you, react calmly and remove yourself from the situation. If that person is a friend or family member, talk to them once they've calmed down about their anger and perhaps discuss where it's coming from and ways of handling it. Sometimes, just talking is enough. Other times some therapy might help.

The worst thing you can do when faced with someone's anger is to allow yours to pique in return. If it does, and you feel you had little control over it, then see the advice above — talk about it once you've calmed down, try to understand it, maybe seek some help to overcome it. Remember: perspective. If someone's angry around you, or at you, they're likely in pain. Pity them, help them if you can. Just don't engage with it until they've had a chance to calm down.

Disagreements

Arguments can knock the stuffing out of you and become a major source of distraction.

The inability to communicate effectively with those who hold a different view has become somewhat endemic lately. John Bercow, erstwhile Speaker of the House of Commons (and bellower of "orderrr!") has spoken about the need for us to learn to "disagree agreeably". It's important to find ways of communicating and thinking about disagreements that minimise their impact on your wellbeing.

We HomeWorkers are more solitary creatures, so are less likely to run into disagreements with irksome colleagues, for example. But when we row with someone at home, then have to go to work in that same space, it can be hard to find the mental separation to cope. The bleed of your home life into your work life is more keenly felt.

If, having had an argument, you find that your focus is affected and you just can't concentrate on work, try going for a walk to get the change of scene and headspace necessary. And as soon as you both can, try to communicate with the other person effectively and in the spirit of reconciliation.

In the throes of a heated disagreement with someone — be it a partner, a loved one or someone else — it can be hard to exercise self-control and good judgement. But do try to remember to communicate your point of view with respect and poise. Don't make the other person feel like you think they're an idiot or evil just because they think differently from you. In fact, go out of your way to ensure that they know this. Say things like "I understand what you're saying," "I do hear you, but…". And never sink to the level of making *ad hominem* remarks, that will get you precisely nowhere.

You can't necessarily avoid arguments, but you can exercise your perspective when it comes to coping with them. Usually, the pain that they cause comes from parts of the psyche that have little do with the fact that one person thinks one thing and another thinks otherwise. Having perspective will make you quicker to understand and to forgive, and it will make you a better communicator.

Perspective On You

Knowing how to think about others and using perspective to handle problematic interactions is one thing, but it's also important to take some time to think about yourself and how your brain works.

Understanding what's going on "under the hood" isn't always easy. But it's important to make the effort to get to know what makes you tick — what triggers you into making poor choices, what drives you to make good ones. You don't have to do this with a therapist, though that would certainly offer you a fuller understanding.

Just spend some time analysing yourself and writing down any thoughts that occur in a stream of consciousness. It doesn't matter what you write — you're the only one who's going to read it back, so be honest with yourself. Try to be neither too complimentary, nor too critical. We're looking for a balanced view of the good and the bad. Tell the truth: what sort of person are you?

Here are some example questions you can ask yourself. The answers you write down will give you a fuller perspective on you, on the decisions you make, and you'll have a clearer picture of how to better manage your wellbeing.

- What motivates me?
- What bores me?
- What distracts me?
- What are my strengths?
- What are some of my bad habits?

- What tends to trigger my bad habits?
- Am I overly self-critical?
- Do I tend to worry about my work?
- Do I plan my time efficiently, or do I bounce from task to task randomly?
- What's my biggest goal for my career?
- Do I have the right mindset about my work?
- If I could snap my fingers and change one thing about my personality, what would it be?
- If I could make everyone else be more like me in one specific way, which of my qualities would I choose?

As a HomeWorker, you're going to be spending an awful lot of time alone, so make sure you enjoy your own company!

Know Thyself

The Myers-Briggs Type Indicator system is world-renowned as a method to determine people's behavioural preferences, and thereby their personality type. Its accuracy lies in the fact that the description it attributes to each "type" of person is based not on their psychological makeup but on their preferences, meaning the behaviour they're most likely to exhibit in any given situation. To put it another way, two people may behave in exactly the same way in a given situation for two completely different reasons, but their preference is nonetheless identical. It's an interesting way to analyse personalities and naturally is used by businesses to study team dynamics, feed into training and help with recruitment. You may have taken one of their tests (a series of multiple choice questions) yourself and found out your type.

You are assigned four letters, each of which is one of a pair. **E**xtroversion or **I**ntroversion, i**N**tuition or **S**ensing, **F**eeling or **T**hinking and **J**udging or

Perceiving. There's no value or judgment placed on whether your preferences tend towards one quality or another within each of the four categories; it's simply a way of understanding how you *tend* to behave, think and make decisions about your life.

The reason I bring Myers-Briggs up is it's a great way to get to know yourself and to think about how HomeWorking might (or might not) be the right choice for you.

For example, if you're an E, you're the kind of person who feels energised and inspired through their interactions with others. You like the constant feedback of having people around to bounce ideas off. Es may struggle with HomeWorking more than Is, who relish the chance to be alone with their thoughts.

This doesn't mean that no E will enjoy HomeWorking (I'm an E, for one!). Nor indeed will you necessarily be cut-out for it just because you're an I. But it's a good way to understand yourself.

Getting a fuller understanding of your character will help you to approach your workdays with insight, realistic expectations and the tact that boss-you needs to show employee-you.

Love Yourself

Yes, it's trite. Yes, it's an overused phrase that appears in a thousand daily Instagram "inspo" posts. But bear with me, this is an important one.

Loving yourself means putting your needs above your compulsions. It's acknowledging that what you *want* to do isn't necessarily what you *need* to do to truly make you happy. Fulfilling the need rather than the compulsion is to put your long-term happiness before short term attraction.

If you're finding that you're easily distracted, *that's* a compulsion. It may feel like you'd rather be doing anything other than work, but if what you want in order to be happy is to achieve your goals, or be financially better off, then doing the work is what you *need* to do.

If you're a people-pleaser, you probably already know that it's behaviour driven by a compulsion (the psychological roots of which could be manifold), and that it can, at times, be sometimes at odds with your own happiness. English chef and writer Nigella Lawson wrote a compelling article about her people-pleasing, and how she makes decisions by asking herself what she'd do if she really loved herself, which helps her stop putting others' needs ahead of her own.

> *FOMO, the fear of missing out, can be a powerful distraction in our social and work lives. My take is that if you're doing anything out of fear, it's usually not a good thing to be doing (apart from running away from danger, obviously). So ask yourself, do you really need to buy that online course, or should you just get cracking with your project? Must you go out to meet friends when, if you were honest with yourself, you'd rather chill at home with your partner? Do you have to buy that thing you're looking at online, or could your pennies be better spent on something that will truly make you happy, like a new book, a vacation or dinner with a loved one? Take my advice, tell FOMO to F-off.*

You may also find that people-pleasing, or not loving yourself enough is affecting your work. If your sense of self-worth is derived exclusively from the approval of others, you're likely to find the isolation of HomeWorking difficult — there's no pat on the back from your boss now. Except, there is...because remember who the boss is? You! You need to pat yourself on the back, and you need for that to be enough. Waiting for affirmations from clients, customers, colleagues or comrades before allowing yourself to feel proud of yourself means you possibly never will.

Takeaways

- Place important emphasis on taking care of your wellbeing.
- Have perspective!
- Learn how to handle difficult personalities in order to avoid stress.
- Get to know yourself and your character.
- HomeWorking may not be for you, and that's OK!
- Love yourself: make positive, proactive choices aimed at increasing your happiness.

MiniWin

Try one of the free versions of the Myers-Briggs test that are online and find out a little more about your personality. It's fascinating!

Then write down 5 changes you could make to your approach to HomeWorking that could better reflect your character traits and preferences.

Next up: how to approach HomeWorking in terms of your diet.

7. HomeWorker Diet

I've found over many years of dieting, eating well, eating poorly, and finally finding a good balance, that what I put in my body has a *huge* effect on what I can put out in terms of energy levels, concentration, alertness and productivity. That's the only angle I'm coming at this from. I don't seek to preach to you about your diet. For one thing, you probably know what's good and what's bad about your dietary habits already. But if making some changes can significantly improve your work life, you're in, right?

Food and Time

This is an important relationship for the HomeWorker in a number of ways. Firstly, it's not about *what* you eat — though that is important — it's about *when* you eat it. We're going to talk about intermittent fasting, and we'll be leaving certain foods out of the diet during the working week. Also, we'll look at managing the time spent preparing food.

Having used myself as a guinea pig for all kinds of diets over the years, I've seen what effect they've had on my working day, and I've now found the one that suits me best and gives me the best results for my body and mind. I lost 26lbs in two months when I switched to this diet, along with exercising regularly. I feel brighter, more focussed, more energetic and able to work with great intensity for longer, which is exactly what's required if you have limited working hours (for instance, I have to down tools at 2.30 pm for the school run!).

There's no office canteen in your home, so one of the many HomeWorking hats you wear is Head of Catering! We aren't going to be buying in ready meals every day (because we want to live), so naturally, you'll be cooking for yourself at home.

You don't want to have to expend too much of your time on feeding yourself during work hours, so lunches in this diet are geared towards meals that are relatively quick and easy to prepare. Perhaps you have ready access to local delis/cafés/restaurants and think that's a quicker and easier way to get hold of meals? Two problems with that: firstly, if you don't want to spend a long time getting hold of food, you're limited to what's nearby, so you'll quickly tire of the available menus. And secondly, it's an expensive way to eat compared to home cooking. As Head of Catering, your job is to provide cheap, quick and nutritious food for your workforce! So, home cooking it is.

Diet Essentials

Here are my HomeWorker Diet essentials…feel free to tweak the rules and recipes to suit your own tastes, but as I say, this works for me!

Intermittent Fasting: Break Your Fast Later in the Morning

If you can get your body used to not expecting food until later, you'll extend your fasting hours, which is, like, really good for you (because science…Google "autophagy"). Essentially, the message is that your body does good, healthy stuff whilst you're fasting, so the longer you can spend in a fasted state each day, the better.

One surefire way to achieve this is to capitalise on the time spent fasting overnight. So try not to snack after dinner and then leave breakfast until later in the morning. You can play with your fasting/feeding times. An easy one to go for is 14 hours of fasting every day. This is achievable if, say, you eat dinner by 8 pm, then don't eat breakfast until after 10 am the following morning. This is a 14/10 fasting/feeding split. This is the pattern I most often follow. As long as I eat dinner by 8 and breakfast after 10, then I'm practicing intermittent fasting most days, without really trying.

You can stretch this out to 16/8 or even 18/6 if you're seeing results and can get used to it. With 18/6, you need to consume all your calories for the day within 6 hours, so say brunch at 12 pm, then an early dinner, finishing by 6 pm. Find what timeframe suits your lifestyle best.

Another approach could be to have lunch later, or skip it entirely. That way you could have your fasting period between an early breakfast at 8am and a later dinner at 10pm.

Because I don't eat breakfast until after 10 o'clock, I'm often not hungry for another big meal until 3 or 4, once the kids are back home. Sometimes, I'll make something light at that time, but more often these days, I'll just have a healthy snack to keep me going. It's only 3 or so hours until dinner, after all.

Don't Eat Carbs During the Week

The sugar crashes caused by carbohydrates are the enemy, especially with few working hours. The last thing I need is to start feeling my energy levels dip right when I've only got an hour or so left of the working day to go. So I stay off carbs during the week, and I seldom, if ever, get the dreaded afternoon lull. Nor do I get the desperate hunger that carbohydrates can give you either, which is also completely distracting. I find I can just work through, feeling the same at 2 pm as I did at 10 am. The effect this has had on my productivity cannot be overstated! If hunger does raise its head, it's a gentle "When you're ready, I'll have some food please, but no rush," as opposed to "Feed me now, or I'll make you murder someone."

Don't Touch "Treaty" Snacks

Crisps, Chocolate, Sweets, Desserts. If you don't know by now that this stuff is best avoided, I'd be amazed. I'm not banning everything, but these 'empty calories' will only serve to make you put on weight, make you unhealthier inside and make your blood sugar spike, then crash. Try to stay off these non-foods until the weekend if you can, and then…have at it, if you like (sorry, nutritionists and diet coaches, I don't need my readers to overhaul their entire diet, I'm just trying to get them through their HomeWorking week!).

Don't Drink Alcohol During the Week

As a lifelong lover of the sauce, this was a difficult one to adopt. Like millions of people, I found that it had become ingrained into my life over the years. Something to celebrate? Let's have a drink. Stressful day? Let's commiserate with a glass of something. It's the weekend? Sure. It's a holiday? Of course! This dinner would go well with wine? Let's open a bottle! I never overdid it in terms of my behaviour, never became an angry drunk, never couldn't do my work the next day, or anything like that. It fitted in with my life tremendously well, which, of course, was the problem, and led to regular over-indulgence.

But eventually, I found a way to stop equating alcohol with reward and see it for what it is: just an unhealthy drink that adds calories to my diet, girth to my middle and removes days from my life expectancy. I see booze in the same way as donuts or ice cream now, which is to say my default is not to indulge. At weekends, sure, but I've managed to reset my intake to come roughly within the government's crazy-hard-to-keep-to limits. Because science, and I want to live.

The benefits you'll feel are massive. No hangovers on weekdays makes early starts easy. You'll concentrate for longer and have more energy. You won't crave unhealthy food. Your bank account will stop straining under your weekly booze budget. Another huge plus for me since dialling down the booze is that I've lost a bajillion pounds in weight!

So again, without being too preachy, if you're someone who's allowed your alcohol intake to get a bit too habitual and knows they should cut back, I advise you to do so before it's too late: you'll find your home and work life both improve immeasurably. I managed to change my habits on my own, but if you need help, there are countless programs out there designed to help you cut down, or stop altogether.

Foods to Fuel You All Day

Now to the diet itself. It will come as no surprise that it has to be made up of healthy, nutritious food. But it also has to include meals that you love to eat, otherwise, you simply won't stick to it day in, day out. This is the key to making it a long-term, sustainable diet. There are lots of options included, so you can make it your own, so long as you stick to the basic principles. Vegetarians and vegans will obviously need to tweak some of my suggestions, for example.

Remember, don't think of it as "going on a diet", recognise that it *is* your diet, then it will simply become part of your daily regimen.

Foods to eat regularly

- Leafy greens like Chinese cabbage, pak choi, spinach, kale, and salad leaves.
- Veg like broccoli, cauliflower, mushrooms, peppers, celery, carrot, onion, beetroot, courgette, green beans, leek.
- Pulses like bean sprouts, edamame, broad beans, lentils.
- Seeds (I have a seed mix that gets sprinkled on pretty much everything).
- Fruits like apples, bananas, berries and, of course, tomatoes, avocado.
- Oily fish like salmon, smoked trout, tinned mackerel.
- Prawns
- Chicken and turkey
- Eggs
- Greek yoghurt (0% fat)

Flavour-enhancing, healthy additions

- Olive oil
- Lemon & lime (zest & juice)
- Fresh garlic
- Fresh root ginger
- Fresh herbs (you can put these on most dishes)
- Chillies (jalapeño is a personal favourite)

Flavour-enhancing less healthy additions (watch how much you put on!)

- Soy sauce, fish sauce
- Hot sauce (sriracha, chipotle)
- Ketchup (the lower sugar & salt kind)
- Mayonnaise (low fat)

Foods to eat less often (and in small quantities during the week)

- Red meat like steak, pork, venison, burgers
- Pasta

- Potatoes
- Veg like peas, sweetcorn, butternut squash
- Bread
- Cheese
- Garlic bread

Foods to avoid in the weeks — save for rare weekend treats!

- Processed meat like sausages, ham, charcuterie, bacon, ribs
- Sugary and salty snacks
- Pizza
- Deep-fried food
- Burgers (when I do have these as a treat, I go all in. They're homemade, rammed with various fillings and *filthy*).

Winning Snacks

- A piece of fruit
- A handful of nuts (almonds and walnuts are especially good for you, unless like my wife you have a nut allergy, that is!)
- Yoghurt with mixed seeds
- Sushi Nori - the dried seaweed that gets wrapped around sushi maki. So tasty & so good for you. Once you get used to the idea of eating dark green paper, you'll love it!
- Crudités & dip: Carrot, celery, pepper, cucumber all make good crudités. Houmous makes a great dip. Take some 0% fat Greek yoghurt and mix in a teaspoon of either spicy chipotle paste, sriracha or a sun-dried tomato pesto to make a dip.
- Kale crisps (no kidding, my kids love these!) just bake for 10 minutes in a light coating of oil & season with salt, pepper & garlic granules.

• Parsnip crips - same principle, just use a speed peeler to shave off strips. Careful with the amount of oil, and don't have too much in the week because parsnips are carb-rich.

Drinks

• Water. Drink it all day, at least 2 litres (about half a gallon). If you need some extra flavour in your water, stay away from the bottled flavoured water with its added sugar or sweeteners. Instead, try an infuser flask - things that work well are cucumber, mint, lemon, lime, orange or watermelon.

• Coffee & tea, in moderation

• No sodas or sugary fruit juices

Example Recipes

Because it's not a cookbook, I'm not giving you too much detail here. These are just a few suggestions pulled from my own go-tos, to inspire you and show you that having healthy, low-calorie meals every day doesn't mean eating boring food. As ever, tweak the recipes to suit your taste.

Breakfast

• Brown smoothie. Mine always come out brown because the base is spinach or kale, banana and mixed frozen berries. And what happens when you mix green, yellow and red? Try to see beyond the colour if you can. It comes out looking like dirty river water, but tastes delicious! I add seed mix and various other fruits like grape, apple, pear or satsuma…whatever's lying around. If it's right after a HIIT session, I'll sometimes stick some porridge oats in to replace lost muscle glycogen. If it's after a run, though, I'll just keep it carb-free.

• Boiled egg, avocado, salad leaves.

• Smoked trout, avocado & cherry tomatoes.

• Japanese rolled omelette, called *tamagoyaki*. For Christmas, my wife bought one of the special rectangular pans used for these delicious, light omelettes, and we have them all the time. Find one of the many YouTube videos that show you how to make them. They're excellent, especially with an *okonomiyaki* sauce made from soy or oyster sauce, Worcestershire sauce and ketchup (you can also add mirin, rice vinegar and sugar, but I just stick to the first three ingredients). You can add finely chopped herbs, onion, carrot, spring onion.

Lunch

• Spinach salad with beetroot, peppers, cherry tomatoes, tinned mackerel in tomato sauce and seed mix.

• Quick tasty Asian broth. It's quick because you don't pre-fry anything, you just put everything into a cold frying pan, add boiling water and then cook it on a medium heat for 5-7 minutes. Ingredients: greens, fresh garlic & ginger, spring onion & carrot cut into strips, sugar snap peas or edamame, frozen prawns, chicken or vegetable stock. Throw the prawns in after a few minutes, and the whole thing's ready as soon as they're cooked. Top with more fresh coriander, spring onion, lime juice and sriracha.

• Chopped salad with feta cheese, peppers, sun-dried tomato, olive, capers.

• Quick veggie stir-fry: peppers, onion, mushroom, sugar snap peas and herbs in a simple soy, ginger and lime sauce.

• Chickpea salad with red onion, avocado and yoghurt & mint dressing.

Dinner

• Chicken caesar salad with kale. Fried chicken thighs in a yoghurt, garlic, anchovy & mustard sauce. Serve with parmesan shavings.

• Prawn burgers. Stick prawns, spring onions, lemongrass, ginger, garlic & coriander in a food processor, form sticky patties and fry them in coconut oil Serve with Asian slaw made from Chinese cabbage and carrot, dressed in yoghurt, peanut butter, soy & lime juice. Also works with turkey or chicken instead of prawn.

- Stir-fry — veggies include pak choi, chinese cabbage, peppers, mushrooms, beansprouts, carrot, spring onion. Meat options are prawn, turkey or chicken. Toppings are sesame seeds, spring onion, fresh coriander, lime juice & sriracha. Try "courgetti" (spiralised courgette) instead of noodles.
- Cheat's ramen or pho. I never quite make these to the traditional recipes, but the principle is: stir-fry some meat & vegetables, add a nice broth made from stock (a stock cube in my case) and serve with fresh herbs, spring onions, sesame seeds and sriracha. You can put a soft-boiled egg on top to finish. Include noodles in the broth if it's a weekend.
- Tacos. A weekend family favourite. We love fish tacos best, but you can use chicken too. Fish can be salmon, cod, pollock, etc. Fish is flavoured with things like paprika, dried coriander & garlic granules and baked in the oven, then flaked. Serve everything else in small bowls and let everyone help themselves. Fillings include pineapple & mango salsa (dry fry the pineapple until it gets some dark colour, then chop and cool before mixing in chopped mango, spring onion, lime juice, fresh mint & chilli); tomato salsa (chopped tomato, fresh garlic, lime juice, red onion, coriander); grated cheese, guacamole, low-fat Greek yoghurt (a swap-out for sour cream) & jalapeños.
- Thai beef salad. One sliced steak serves two people. Make a dressing out of lime juice, garlic, lemongrass, soy sauce, fish sauce & chilli. Marinate the steak in some of the dressing before frying. Serve it on a bed of crispy lettuce with beansprouts and the rest of the dressing. Top with chopped peanuts or cashews and sliced spring onion.

Top Tip for Reluctant Cooks: ***Mise-en-place***

People I've spoken to who dislike home cooking often cite the mess and chaos that can be created by following a recipe. The best way to combat this is to have an organised approach.

The French culinary term *mise-en-place* (literally "putting in place") is the way to go. Read the whole recipe, get little bowls or ramekins out ready with all your ingredients before you cook, along with all the necessary equipment. You'll be more organised, and feel like you're about to present a cooking show on TV!

Another tip: clean up as you go. If you leave everything until the end, you'll have a messy kitchen to handle when all you want to do is eat your meal. Also, the thought of that mess will make you less likely to want to repeat the experience in the future. But regularly "clearing down" as you go will mean there's minimal washing up by the time you're ready to eat.

Meal Prep

The internet seems to be awash these days with photos of food in multiple Tupperware boxes. You've probably seen some. This is the phenomenon known as "prepping" your meals in advance, often portioning out an entire week's worth of meals. Batch cooking like this is a good idea, and saves both time and money. I must admit I seldom do this, however, as I happen to enjoy cooking, so depriving myself of that unwinding, creative activity everyday would be a negative. For those who don't want to be bothered with this during the working week, preparing everything in advance — on Sunday night, say — will be a positive.

Takeaways

- Not too many takeaways (see what I did there?).
- Practice intermittent fasting - it saves time and is good for you.
- Snack wisely.
- No carbs in the week.
- Save treats for weekends.
- Use quick-to-make recipes for workday lunches.
- Prep your meals in advance.
- Before cooking, *mise-en-place.*

MiniWin

Write yourself a meal plan for your lunches this week. Think about prep time and whether you can plan in leftovers from dinners.

Here's an example week with 5 quick and healthy meals types for you to adapt to your tastes:

Monday - leftover Sunday night curry (leave the rice for low carb option)
Tuesday - Fish, meat or pulses with a leafy salad
Wednesday - Quick Asian broth (see above)
Thursday - Chopped salad
Friday - Veggie stir-fry

8. HomeWorker **Body**

Let me be clear, we're not going to be talking about the way your body **looks** here, but how it **functions.** Specifically, how you can keep your energy high throughout the day and enjoy long-term physical health.

I've learned lots over the years about how (and how not) to look after my physical wellbeing. Unless you're a fitness instructor, the chances are that your HomeWorking mostly involves using your brain, not your body. Well, here's a fact you simply can't get around: your brain is inside a human body that needs to be looked after. If your body's *not* being cared for, fuelled and exercised properly, your brain can't function to its full capacity.

THINK OF IT LIKE THIS: YOU DON'T HAVE YOUR BODY, YOU *ARE* YOUR BODY.

So looking after it, staying healthy, keeping energised and preventing **downtime** due to illness or injury is absolutely part of your remit as a HomeWorker.

Exercise

Our bodies — sadly, I hear some of you thinking — are designed to be used. Frequently. We're evolved from people who needed to walk the savannah all day to forage for food, climb trees, and have the fitness both to chase after whatever they were hunting, and to run away to from anything that wanted to hunt them. Sitting down for hours and staring at a screen was never on our DNA's agenda. Nor were refined sugars and pies!

So, as well as controlling your diet, you have to trick your body into thinking it's on the savannah, by exerting it. Daily if you can.

I'm no fitness guru. My physical exercise has consisted mainly of tennis in my teens and running in my thirties. But I long ago made exercise a regular part of my life, and I've learned some stuff worth passing on, no matter what age you are.

I spent lots of my twenties as a couch potato when I wasn't working. I was kind of into running, a bit, but not regularly. What did I care? My metabolism was taking care of all the crap I threw at it. And I had plenty of time to make progress in my work, didn't I? What did it matter if I woke up hungover one morning and spent the day watching TV before my next teaching gig? I could afford to, right?

I'm sure you can detect the sarcasm. One of my biggest regrets (and frustrations) is that I didn't live then the way I live now. I'd have been healthier, more energetic, and way more productive. Well, I can't change that, but I can advise you to make the most of these tips in order to…no, I can't say it…I shan't…no, you can't make me! In order to…"live your best life."

Ugh, I feel dirty.

In all seriousness, that over-used and trite phrase does have some useful meaning for HomeWorkers, if you simply take it to mean this: that you're putting yourself in the best position possible to stay healthy and happy in the short, medium and long-term, and be capable of working towards your goals at your maximum capacity without any negative impact on your wellbeing. But sure, "live your best life" is catchier.

Today, Millennials are very aware of their diet, of working out, of the importance of self-care and wellbeing and mental health and goal setting. Well done, Millennials. (And, if you are a Millennial, before you "OK, boomer" me, I'm actually a "Xennial". Look it up).

For those of us who are a little older and who weren't barraged day and night with self-improvement posts, ads and YouTube videos from a young age, it can be a bit trickier to update our lifestyle and routines. But it's eminently possible, believe me.

And you'll see fantastic results.

What You'll Experience When You Exercise Regularly

I'm sure you know what all the other benefits of regular (and I do mean regular!) exercise are, but they're worth repeating:

- Improved focus. Since moving to a 5-a-week regime, I've found that my energy is *way* higher than it was, and I can concentrate for longer periods of time.

- Improved musculoskeletal strength and flexibility, which assists with things like bad backs from sitting in a chair all day.
- Great stress-buster. Feeling anxious? Workout, and the adrenalin levels will decrease.
- Better sleep, which means a better you!
- You'll live longer.
- You'll look better (I've lost 36lbs to date doing this — haven't been this weight for a decade!)
- You'll feel worthy, well, and proud to have ticked another thing off for the day. I see my half-hour run as a big win, every day.

So I'm sorry if you hate it, but unless you do it, you won't be able to max-out your planner because your body won't be able to keep up with the work demands you place on it. My advice to reluctant exercisers is: start small. A quick 10 minute walk is a great start. Then gradually increase over time.

If you're interested in maximising productivity, the question of whether to make exercise part of your day is a choice between: a) getting less done, feeling lethargic and being unhealthy, or b) getting lots done, feeling great and having a healthier body. It's a no-brainer when you think of it like that, right?

Keep on Running

When I was 28, and my mum's breast cancer returned, I decided to run the London Marathon to raise money for a breast cancer charity. I'd been running a few time before, but never regularly. It was the first time I'd trained properly. By the time the Marathon came and went I'd spent six months training, running four or five times a week, sometimes for up to three hours at a time. Running had become a part of my life, so I kept it going.

There have been some periods when I've stopped running regularly, and I never quite feel right until I get back in the habit again. But I've mostly managed to keep it going, including the odd 10K and Half Marathon race. It suits me.

So now, because I'm trying to exercise Monday to Friday, for 30 minutes a day, I run. Only when the weather is abysmal will I reluctantly stay home and do some high-intensity interval training (HIIT) or strength training with a kettlebell, dumbbell or body weight workout. My wife's even gotten me into a bit of yoga. But for me, running works best, and I find it's something I can stick to every day. In 30 minutes, I run around 5K (3 miles), just over 500 calories burned a day, sorted.

The point here is to find your ideal exercise routine. It could be that you despise running and prefer cycling. Or perhaps you hate cardio and would rather do strength training or lift weights. Maybe you're a yogi through and through! The most important thing for the purposes of this book is that you need to find your own exercise regimen, one that you can commit to and make part of your life forever.

Fitting it in

I used to struggle with justifying the time it took to exercise because it felt like getting to work was more important, especially once we had children and my work time became slightly more scant (and, therefore, even more precious). Two things helped with this: 1. waking early and 2. keeping workouts to 30 minutes or less. I also came to accept that when I exercise, I'm so much more productive for the rest of the day than if I haven't, so I can't afford *not* to invest the time to fit it in.

If you have limited time during the day (for example, like me you're bound by the school run), then you'll have to choose your exercise wisely. For me, anything which takes me away from home (and, therefore, my work) for any longer than absolutely necessary, is a no-no. This rules out going out to the gym or swimming pool, both of which involve too much time being spent either side of the exercise.

The workouts which work best if you're trying to squeeze them in are anything you can do either at home, or from home. So that includes home workouts like HIIT training, yoga or pilates and going for a walk, cycle or run from your house. There are some wonderful running routes in my area, but unless I wanted to spend the entire 30 minutes running through town to reach them, they're all a drive away. Even a 5-minute drive would add up to 50 minutes a week of lost work time (there and back, Monday to Friday), so I keep my running to the local park, which, mercifully, is right next door.

You don't need lots of time or space to exercise, just a daily habit that fits around your schedule and suits your environment.

You don't have to program in a full 30 minutes all at once in order to get your exercise in, you can squeeze in mini-workouts throughout the day. For example, when we lived in a big house in Belgium (it's a long story), every day, I would run up to the third floor where we had an exercise area and do 50 sit-ups and 10 press-ups. It took all of 4 minutes, and I did this at least 4 times a day, totalling 200 sits-ups and 40 press-ups.

The benefit of chunking it up like this made it easier than committing to a 20-minute workout. Also, it meant that I was running up the two flights of stairs 4 times instead of just once. And it was a guaranteed break time away from my desk and screen, which benefited my eyes, posture, energy and concentration.

And what was my cue to go do this? How did I spread it throughout the day? Well, I set a habit that each time I went to the bathroom, I had to go do a set! If you're not going to the bathroom at least 4 times during a workday, you're probably not drinking enough water - 2 litres, (half a gallon) a day is recommended, remember.

This routine worked for me for about a year, but now I favour the "getting it all done early" approach, so I exercise in the morning and enjoy not having to worry about it for the rest of the day, not to mention the positivity boost I feel having fitted in the early win.

Whatever you do for exercise, try out a few different approaches and see what works for you. This means finding things that you can successfully incorporate into your daily routine, and stick to.

Other Considerations

Don't forget to stretch throughout the day, don't stay in one position at your desk for too long and stand up every so often (my Apple Watch reminds me to do this — in a rather imperious fashion, I feel).

Have a think about the **ergonomics** of your desk set up. Chair, desk height, keyboard, mouse, where you write. If you're not comfortable every day, you can't work to your best, and you might cause your body damage (back pain, neck strain, RSI in your wrists, etc.).

You shouldn't be feeling any soreness or stiffness after a work session. If you are, adjust your set up, so you aren't hunching, twisting or leaning.

Takeaways

- Build regular exercise into your daily routine — preferably every workday.
- Sleep regular hours.
- Have a comfortable workspace.
- Stretch, take breaks and move throughout the day.

MiniWins

Write down one of the following HomeWorker Body goals and focus on working towards it for a month:

- Lose 10lbs.
- Start running (or set a goal distance to work towards, like 5K/3 miles or 10K/6 miles).
- Do 3 x home workouts per week — all you need is an exercise mat and YouTube!

When the month is up, track how well you did and come up with a new goal.

9. HomeWorker **Mindset**

So you're eating right, you're exercising, you've got a good self-care plan in action to look after your mental wellbeing. You're organised. What's left? Your **mindset**.

Mindset is a buzzword. Mindset is motivation. It's discipline. It's a winning mentality. You can acknowledge all the tips and tactics in this book, even put some of them into practice, but unless you develop a winning mindset, the chances are you might lose momentum or revert to old (bad) habits.

You might not be someone who's naturally blessed with a mentality to chase down success. Don't be offended if that's you, you're probably a lot happier than those who are. Many successful people got that way because their mental makeup wired them up in such a way that they feel they *have* to prove themselves, *have* to win. Much as this may lead them to create successes in their lives that do, in part, contribute to their satisfaction and contentment, you can't really say that it all comes from a place of happiness.

I'm not like that, not really. I'm ambitious, sure. But I'm not someone who'll give up everything, including my own wellbeing and happiness — or that of those around me — to be successful. Nor am I saying that everyone who is successful is necessarily like that.

There are many psychology books and personal growth manuals out there that go into this in greater detail. For the purposes of our journey together, my only wish is to give you the perspective to consider what's really important to you, and to balance your HomeWorking career goals with the goals you should have for your own wellbeing.

Motivation & Responsibility

People often rely on outside sources to give them motivation, like:

- Inspirational quotes
- Uplifting videos on YouTube
- Personal trainer
- Life coach
- Comparing oneself to others (celebrities, friends, heroes)
- Books (like this one!)

These sources can be a piece of the puzzle, for sure, and you can derive immense motivation from them.

But…that motivation can be short-lived.

ONLY ONE PERSON CAN *KEEP* YOU MOTIVATED: YOU.

Me

You have to find a way to cultivate your own HomeWorker mindset so that you can actually do this every day: work well and remain happy and balanced. It won't just come, you have to work at it.

There are a thousand books, websites and channels about the power of harnessing your mindset. But really, it comes down to two simple questions:

1. What do you want, and what are you prepared to do to get it?
2. Will the pursuit of this dream allow you to remain healthy, stable and content?

Once you know what the answer to Question 1 is, and *only* if you're sure the answer to Question 2 will be "yes," you can ask yourself this important question:

3. Are you prepared to **take responsibility** for yourself?

I've been thinking about the last one a lot recently. Young people today are often accused of being things like "entitled snowflakes", but actually I think they're the ones who really are taking responsibility for themselves. Drinking amongst young people is going down, smoking's rare, veganism's on the rise and they're far more switched on about global issues like political divides and climate change than previous generations have been, mine included.

As I mentioned before, I'm a Xennial, an inbetweener. We grew up with computers and are at ease with both the Technology and Information Revolutions but are still old enough to have enjoyed cassettes, Walkmans and Life Before The Internet).

If like me, you were born before 1980, you may be less immersed in the culture of wellbeing than those born later. You might not even have *heard* the word "wellbeing" (at least, not with any regularity) until a few years ago.

You may even struggle with the idea of "self-improvement" or "personal growth". Self-help books used to be the butt of jokes: the purview only of eccentric New Age weirdos and dropouts. But in the last twenty years, they've grown more "normalised", and it's quite rational now to buy a book that teaches you to do something better. That is, after all, what *this* book is for!

Nowadays, people are more willing to learn new things at any age, and since we're in the Information Revolution that's become much easier. We now have the ability, if we choose, to advance our ongoing personal development and education ourselves. However it takes some commitment to do this under our own steam. Often it would be easier not to show such determination and drive.

You don't *have* to self-improve. You do have a choice. But people who are serious about achieving both success *and* balance must accept that while we may not like being grown-ups and having to take responsibility, take responsibility we must.

Commitment & Discipline

Discipline's a word that comes up a lot in this book. If you lack it, there's no career that will show this up more than HomeWorking, where you're, strictly speaking, not directly accountable to anyone but yourself.

I wasn't always disciplined, but I realised — as most do — that you can learn to be. And this comes from the dissatisfaction one feels after a period of not getting things done, or not achieving one's goals. We *wish* we could be more disciplined. We *desire* the feeling of achievement.

The best way I found to develop my discipline was by making **commitments** to myself. As with a loving relationship, if you truly commit to something, then it becomes a part of who you are, and working to maintain or improve it isn't a chore, it's something you've elected to do for your own sake, because the alternative is letting it slide or losing it altogether.

That's where discipline comes from: not from sheer will power but from having gained the perspective that whatever challenges you face in working towards a goal, it is far preferable to face them than not to achieve it.

In his book *Indistractable*, Nir Eyal learned that the internal triggers that can lead us to be distracted actually occur as a function of our desire to avoid pain. Not to seek pleasure, to avoid pain. He argues that evolutionarily speaking, that's always been a far greater motivator than anything else and is hard-wired into us. If you apply this logic not only to your productivity but also to your career/health/fitness goals, you'll gain new insight into how to stay disciplined.

Think about it like this:

The thought: ***I want to be successful*** actually comes from impulses and neuroses related to: ***I don't want to be poor/disappoint my parents/be seen as a loser.***

I want to lose weight is really: ***I don't want to be fat/look bad/die early.***

I want to clean the house/play a game/check Instagram instead of working comes from: ***I'm scared I'll fail/I don't want to do a bad job/this work might be hard.***

You get the idea.

So the best way to stay disciplined is to think about the **pain** involved in **not doing** what you know you need to do. And in terms of your career, you need to paint yourself a picture of what **not** achieving your dreams, goals and ambitions looks like. You may already have an idea because it's what life is like now. Or you may love your work so much that the thought of losing it is too painful to think about.

When you start doing these little thought experiments and use them to adapt your attitude in this way, you soon begin to develop discipline because the alternative is too **painful**.

You might think this sounds like a depressing, negative way to look at things, but it's quite the reverse. Once you develop discipline and learn to stay motivated, stick to your plan, follow through, meet your goals, finish projects, lose weight, get up early, anything…the sense of pride and satisfaction you'll feel makes this way of approaching life an overwhelmingly positive and fulfilling one.

Takeaways

- Take responsibility for your own progress and get serious about discipline.
- Commit to routines and force compliance by acknowledging your primary motivation: to avoid pain!

• Set reasonable, achievable goals and reward MiniWins.

MiniWin

Write down something you've longed to achieve for ages, even something not related to your HomeWorking career, like learning a language or taking dance classes or dropping a few pounds. Then write down what winning looks like (i.e., make it measurable). For example, "learn 1000 Spanish words" or "lose 10 pounds" or "learn a tango routine from scratch."

Then imagine what your life will be like if you do it. And what about if you **don't do it?** Hold on to the second part of that question, what life will be like if you **avoid** chasing this goal.

Then spend a month doing it. Really commit to it. Avoid the pain of not doing it!

Then, having achieved your goal, ask yourself the question again: what's your life like now you've done it? What would life be like **if you hadn't?**

You see? Think about pain avoidance as a motivation tool…it's a very positive way to think!

10. HomeWorker Goals

Goal-setting is the practice of stating to yourself what specific things you want to achieve in your life and work, and measuring your progress towards achieving them.

What Should Your Goals Be?

There's a wealth of information out there about how to use goal setting to make progress in your professional life. It's a good idea to plan in some goals, maybe to have some monthly, yearly targets. Having a five or a ten year plan is popular. I think these can all be useful thought experiments and help you begin to dig down into what you want to achieve.

A word of caution, though: goals are not the goal. By which I mean that writing down a goal and then ticking it off once you've achieved it is only part of the story. Think of goals as targets, as milestones to reach, as a useful tool. They are the pegs on which you hang your planning and scheduling, and a yardstick by which you can measure progress.

DON'T think of them as the be-all-and-end-all of creating and tracking your success and happiness.

Why Goals Aren't Helpful

Sorry to be the bearer of bad news, but the majority of your "life goals" (if you have them) won't actually make you happy. They just won't. But that's no reason not to have them.

Most of us have goals. At the very least, it's a wish list of stuff we want from our lives. It might be actual stuff, as in: "I want to buy my dream car," or "I want to own a house in Malibu." Other times it's a wish to achieve something, as in: "My goal is to be a millionaire by the time I'm 30," or "I want to draw cartoons for a living."

Some people aren't built like that, of course. Their life goals, if they even have them, are limited, often being informed by what they've already got. Some of these people get to a point where they're happy to just continue as they are. They accept the things about their life that they wish were different but know (or think) they can't change, and simply concentrate on enjoying the rest. They just live on. Some of these people are possibly the happiest people in the world.

I'm going to make an assumption now: that's not you. For a start, someone like the person I just described wouldn't be reading a book designed to help them improve their lives by learning and trying out new things. Those happy people have no need of aspiration, for what is there to aspire to, if you're already happy with your lot?!

That doesn't mean that the rest of us are miserable, though. We just, perhaps haven't found the right balance yet, or achieved everything we want to. We might know (or suspect) what needs to change about our lives — both professional and personal — in order to make us happier.

Whatever the extent of their personal and professional ambition is, HomeWorkers (and those considering doing it) tend by nature to be inquisitive, thoughtful, self-reflecting people, who are willing to think differently from the norm. They consider new possibilities, take roads less travelled; they take responsibility for their progress towards their goals and will try all kinds of new techniques to achieve them. They're prepared to work in unconventional careers and face the dreaded "So what do *you* do?" question with patience and poise.

We've already talked about how HomeWorkers (with the exception of remote staff working for an existing company) have to plan their own day. The same is true of your goals. People with bosses have things they want to achieve with their career too, but this must always be balanced with what their boss wants them to achieve, what their team needs them to get done, and what the pre-defined paths through the company's hierarchy might be.

HomeWorkers get to decide much more of our day for ourselves. The downside? We have to decide much more for ourselves!

But it does mean that we frequently visualise goals for our career, our lives, our health and our families. This is great, and if that's an instinct that comes naturally to you, I would never advise against setting goals. Just please, please don't pin your dreams of a happy life on any of them.

The Only Goal That Matters

The one and only goal to pursue (relentlessly, daily, endlessly) is happiness. That's the only thing worth aiming for, *for its own sake*. Everything else is just a target at which to throw a dart in the hope that hitting the bullseye will somehow make life better. People can devote years of their life to toil, agony, sacrifice and pain in the pursuit of goals they mistakenly believe will "come good" for them one day, without ever learning how to be happy today.

There's a reason I called this book *The Happy HomeWorker*. When thinking about your HomeWork — your goals, your work/life balance, your daily routines — I truly believe that you should place equal emphasis on your wellbeing and happiness as you do on achieving your career goals. If not more.

But even if you have the perspective to make the pursuit of happiness your life's mission, does that mean you'll achieve it? Is anyone ever truly happy? The answer to this is, quite possibly, "no". But it doesn't mean you shouldn't prioritise this goal above all others. Besides, there are ways of thinking about your happiness that will make achieving it entirely feasible.

But first, let's look at what happiness *is*. Nice easy question to tackle, I know. But let's give it a go.

What *is* Happiness?

Age, specifically in the sense of it being an aggregate of experience, naturally teaches you things. How many people want the same things at 30 they did at 20? How about when they're 40? 50? As our circumstances change, so do our dreams; therefore so must our goals and our definition of happiness. For most of my 20s and 30s, I was fairly conscious of what I wanted from my career and thought a lot about my life goals. It ended up boiling down to one thing: I want to earn money from writing music. Now in my 40s, having done that to varying degrees in a few different spheres of the industry, I'm glad to have done it. But there's that little voice that says, "OK, you've done that, so what's next?"

Some think that voice is called ambition, something driving us forward to build on our achievements, to keep *improving*. Perhaps, but I think it's more than that. It's the part of us that seeks reward, or, more accurately (as we discussed in the previous chapter) to avoid pain. Before you achieve a specific goal, you assume (maybe correctly) that by achieving it, you'll get a certain reward, like better finances, emotional fulfilment, getting respect and recognition from peers or family. But the thing is, *even if* you get those things — and feel great about them for a while — that voice will always be there, asking for more. You want more reward, more things to fix you, to comfort you, to assuage those drives and desires that come from all parts of our psyche, both the good and the bad, the light and the dark.

That voice won't let you enjoy your achievement for long, if at all. It will simply ask, "What's next?"

You shouldn't listen to that voice. At least, you shouldn't let it govern your every important career and life decision.

Why?

Because **we're usually not the best judges of what makes us truly happy** day-in, day-out.

We assume that getting to the finish line of whatever path we set for ourselves (or is set for us by others) will be the thing that triggers happiness. How many times have you started a sentence with the following words?

- If only...
- Wouldn't it be great just to...

- Life would be so much better if…
- All I need is…
- I'd be happier if…
- I'll be happy when…

The sentiments that follow these opening phrases are often your current life goals. Here are some examples:

- If only **I could work part-time.**
- Wouldn't it be great just to **go and travel more?**
- Life would be so much better if **we lived in X.**
- All I need is **more time.**
- I'd be happier if **I lost twenty pounds.**
- I'll be happy when **I've reached $10,000 income a month/got my dream car/ married someone/had kids/retired.**

These are all perfectly reasonable desires, and if you have any of them as your goals, know this: achieving them would probably improve your life, which would, in turn, increase your happiness, to a degree. **However**, don't fall into the trap of thinking that any one of these will make you consistently content on a daily basis. If they did, everyone who'd achieved their goals would be happy all the time. Look around at the people in your life…is there anyone who achieved a goal, and the achievement of it *in and of itself* has resulted in their being constantly fulfilled? Do you really know anyone who exudes this perma-joy?

Of course not. Because we're human. We're balls of hopes, dreams, fears, neuroses, flaws, jealousies, pride and avarice. And we're all different. Anyone who says there's a simple universal way of making us all happy is lying, a fool and probably after your money.

We're not designed to be happy; we're designed to survive and procreate. Happiness is a nice byproduct of living, not its chief goal, (at least, not as far as evolution is concerned). That means that whilst our conscious minds might well seek happiness, our unconscious minds (controlled by our inner natures) can lead us to impulses that may not serve our conscious goals.

So how *can* we be happy, at least as much as we are able to be, inside our messed-up little monkey brains?

The best answer I've come up with over my 40-odd years on the planet is: **by ensuring our own regular contentment.**

Not happiness — contentment. Happiness is ineffable, nebulous and fickle. Contentment is simply a good feeling. It releases good chemicals inside us. No matter how transient it may be, a day when we've felt contentment is a day we've got something to latch onto, so we can tell ourselves, "this good thing happened today."

This is key, though: it has to be fairly easily-achievable. So, for example, saying "I'm content when I'm on holiday" won't cut it since you probably can't achieve this on a weekly basis. We're looking for realistic, regularly-occurring things that make you feel good.

As far as your HomeWork goes, this means you should aim for it to include something that you derive pleasure from doing. It can't *all* be a gas (most of us hate bookkeeping, for example!), but so long as enough of it fulfils and enriches your day, you can say it makes you content. Then you'll begin to focus less on end goals and derive pleasure and satisfaction from the work itself. Over to you, Will:

THINGS WON ARE DONE; JOY'S SOUL LIES IN THE DOING.

William Shakespeare

Perfect.

The other part of the equation is that when we take responsibility for ensuring our own contentment, we're **doing it for ourselves.**

This is good for two reasons:

1. If you rely on others for your contentment, whether or not you feel it on any given day will depend on the day they're having, what their mood is, how available they are. Take responsibility for this task yourself, and you know *you'll* always show up for it.
2. Once you've done something, or made a choice that's ensured your contentment, even for a brief spell, you own that action. *You* did it. You made your life better. Very little feels better than that, and the pride you feel will reinforce and augment your contentment.

And here's the good news: as HomeWorkers, we are best-placed to do this because we ourselves are responsible for large parts of our time, and which things we want to focus on.

My advice to you is to analyse what makes you content, figure out what achievable action will bring that contentment about, and put that action into your daily or weekly plan.

Here are some examples:

I feel content when:	Action to achieve this:
I see my weight go down on the scales	Eat better, exercise more
I've written something	Write something. Every day.
I eat a lovely dinner with my partner	Cook/Plan a date night!
I'm hugged by a love one	Ask for a hug from someone you love
I've got lots of work done and can relax in the evening	Plan your day efficiently and work hard

So, by all means, set some goals. But please don't attach too much importance to the achieving of them *for their own sake*. Have a wider, more holistic, and all-encompassing sense of your path through life, and make it your purpose (whatever your goals are) to ensure your own regular contentment. It won't make you happy all of the time, but it will ensure that the sum of your life will add up to many days where you felt good about something, and enjoyed the experience of living.

And I think that's as valid a definition of happiness as any.

So, with that in mind, you can go forwards into the days, weeks, months and years ahead with a refreshed perspective (there's that word again).

Phew. Well, now that we've solved the ineffable question of how to be happy(!), we can return to more prosaic concerns like how best to approach structuring your daily routine.

I mean, happiness is one thing, but you still have a job to do!

The Power of Routine

Your daily routine has two facets. One is experiential, which is to say tha what you experience every day adds up to your experience of life. If you're goin to do something regularly, daily, you'd better think about the ways in which i builds towards your happiness. And, remember, though it's perfectly valid to d something every day that you don't *necessarily* love doing (but is required t achieve your long-term goals) it's also important to include things that ensur regular contentment.

The second facet of routine is its function as a method to achieve the goal you've set out to achieve. By which I mean that doing things routinely can ad up to big result over time, which is why it's important to foster good habits.

Building Good Habits

The way to ensure your progress is to build habits that become second nature to the point that your will power becomes irrelevant.

Take exercise, for example. The only way I've been able consistently t exercise every weekday is by making it part of my daily routine, at the same tim every day. Which is to say, when it gets to that time, it's exercise time. I don' have to ask questions, I don't have to weigh the benefits or think about th consequences (because as soon as I do, I'll begin to bargain with myself and fin reasons *not* to exercise). The physical struggle to begin exercising is hard enough sometimes, without adding all that mental wrangling. I just have to do it because that's my routine. Then it's done, and I've hardly had to think about it.

The same thing goes for eating healthily, or going to bed on time. Am I going to eat carbs today? No, it's a Tuesday. Will I go to bed before 10.30? Yeah, because tomorrow's Wednesday and the alarm will go off at 5. Easy.

Habit Tracking

A great way to establish and curate a set of daily habits is to use a habit tracker. There are several apps out there that do this, but I find that using a simple spreadsheet is just as effective.

The importance of tracking habits lies in the act of tracking itself, because when you log having successfully completed something that you hope to do daily, it feels good. Then, when you manage to do it again the next day, you start to build up a streak. Your habit tracker will become a record of how well you've done and will also motivate you by disincentivising the breaking of your streak. It becomes a game, albeit a serious one.

You might break that streak, for some reason. That's OK. If you do, get straight back on the horse and start a new streak tomorrow. Look forward, not back.

Once you've completed a long enough streak, you'll be able to look back and realise that your daily habit has become part of your everyday life. It takes a good couple of months for a habit to really become ingrained — 66 days, according to a study done at University College London. It will be quicker for some habits, slower for others.

CHANGE COMES IN EXCRUCIATING INCREMENTS FOR THOSE WHO WANT IT.

Josiah Bartlet, The West Wing.

True. But even so, if it's positive change, it's still worth attaining. The way to make the increments less excruciating is to hide them inside daily habits that you don't notice. Over time, the results add up.

HomeWorker Habits

After years of honing, I've got a few daily habits that are now hard-wired into my weekly work routine (which, in my case, runs from Monday to Friday).

My daily habits are:

- Waking early: 5 am starts for the win!
- Exercise: 5 x 30minutes per week, usually a 5K (3 mile) run.
- Reading: Books, articles, blogs, essays. Social media feeds don't count!
- Deep breathing: Sometimes I'll do a full meditation or deep breathing routine, but more often I just take some deep breaths for a minute or so. Works wonders.
- Stretching: Not necessarily the kind that requires a yoga mat, just some chair-based or standing stretches to help keep muscle soreness and back pain away.

Have a think about what other habits you might consider incorporating into your daily routine. Learning something new for 10 minutes, perhaps. Or going for a walk after work (the "fake commute").

Once you've selected the habits you want to begin, start doing and tracking them. Stick with it, even when it's tough. But also recognise that certain habits just aren't destined to stick to you. That's OK, too. If you've tried something and are certain you've given it your maximum tenacity, and it *still* isn't providing you with the value or results you want, then scratch it off your habits list and think of a new one to try.

Keep experimenting until you find your list of "non-negotiables". Those are your daily habits.

Takeaways

- Place as much emphasis on your happiness as you do on your career, if not more.
- Pursue your long term goals, but also ensure your regular contentment along the way.
- Accept that many of your bigger goals will probably change over time.
- Accept that you won't necessarily meet every goal. Make new goals.
- Curate and commit to some "non-negotiable" daily habits.

MiniWins

1. Write out what makes you content and what action will achieve that end. Then take the actions and put them in your daily planner. No matter how

densely-packed your schedule is, fit in at least one contentment-creating action per day.

I feel content when:	Action to achieve this:

2. Brainstorm a few habits that you think would benefit you. Make them small and easily-achievable. Then begin incorporating them into your daily routine, tracking them in a spreadsheet, and see which ones you can easily stick to. After a month, begin building on those habits, by lengthening the time spent on them or expanding their scope.

11. The Long Term: A Career and a Life as a HomeWorker

So, have I put you off yet?!

Hopefully not. I hope the advice in this book has made you see what a great thing HomeWorking can be for you, as long as you're aware of the challenges and take responsibility for planning your approach to tackle them.

Getting it right is the best kind of win because it's entirely personal and self-initiated. The pride you'll feel in achieving your goals when you work under your own steam far outweighs the feeling you get from a boss giving you a figurative pat on the back.

You've gotten this far through the book (thanks!), and that means you've spent time working out the following things:

- What your business model should be.
- How to implement it.

- What your personal and professional goals are.
- You're aware of the need to care for your wellbeing.
- You've decided to make exercise part of your life.
- You've elected to prep and home cook healthy meals.
- You've committed to maintaining a regular sleep pattern.
- You have the right mindset and discipline to succeed.
- You understand more about happiness, and how to establish routines and habits that foster it.

So what's next?

You just bloody get on with it, that's what's next. But you knew that already.

That sad time — one I know so well — is approaching: when the training manual, video or (in this case) book is drawing to a close. It's almost imparted all its wisdom and advice, and now the onus is squarely back on **you;** it's time to get to it! You're now going to have to put what you've learned into practice and actually do the work. But hopefully, now that you've read the book, the former will help with the latter.

I'm easing you in though; there's still a little more advice to come.

Below are some closing thoughts and considerations

Remember: It's Your Home, Too

You need to balance your work life with your home life, which means not putting one before the other. In the rush to create the perfect workspace and maximise your working productivity, it can be easy to forget that you live here too. In many cases, so do others.

Your home can have a section that you utilise as a workspace, but that does not mean it's an office in which you sometimes live; it's a house in which you sometimes work. Respect that your home's primary function is to be just that: a home.

Tidiness isn't just about keeping a well-ordered workspace to help productivity. It helps with mental calmness too. Make sure your workspace doesn't begin to encroach on the rest of your home, or if it does during working hours, be sure to tidy it all away when work is done. This is made easier if you're able to achieve complete separation of work and living spaces.

Knowing when to take a day for yourself, as mentioned above, is important. But sometimes, you'll just need to take one — or a portion of one — for the house! Do try to keep housework to non-working hours if you can, but sometimes, things will build up to the point where you just need to commit some time to get the place ship-shape again.

Recently, my wife was away with work for a week and I was handling the kids and my HomeWork, as usual. It coincided with one of those weeks where the house was beginning to require a bigger clean. Usually, we'd spend time at the weekend doing this, but this week was different. The day she was returning was Valentine's day. So, being an old romantic, I thought the best present I could give her (on top of flowers of course, I'm not a moron) would be that when she returned, exhausted and jet-lagged after her trip, she'd walk into a nice clean house, and we wouldn't have to spend any time doing housework over the weekend. Well, as a HomeWorker, I was able to take a day off to do this.

It's also important to be respectful of those around you if you live with family or have roommates. Communicate clearly with them about what you need, especially if you're on a project that's going to require longer-than-usual working hours. Also, listen to what they have to say about how your HomeWorking affects them. Come to a compromise for how you're going to approach your home/work balance for the benefit of everyone who lives under the same roof. If everyone understands what everyone else's expectations are in advance, friction and fallings out will be minimised.

Communicate with others, too: be clear with your clients and customers what your working hours are, especially if they don't match the traditional 9-5. Manage their expectations so that you don't end up committing to a deadline for them that will completely throw your home/work/life balance out of whack. For example, I recommend being honest about the school run. My clients know that I'm "out of office" from 2.30 pm. But because I work early mornings and some evenings, I know my output easily matches that of someone working regular hours.

> ***Cautionary Tale: Double Screening!*** *Just because technology allows you to work at any time, it doesn't mean you should! During my crazy period working the equivalent of three jobs, I experienced the feeling that many of us do, which is that I was never quite on top of everything that needed doing. So I would triage things for "later". This inevitably meant taking care of non-urgent emails on the sofa when my wife and I were together of an evening. It quickly became clear that not only was I missing out on time with her to unwind and decompress, I was also making her feel neglected. This was a red line for us both, and I quickly put this practice out to pasture! I do still double screen at times, but it's not usually for work. More likely, it will be to browse social media or catch up with friends, both of which I avoid doing during work hours. But there's also value in just putting your phone or tablet down and focussing on one thing, whether it's conversation with your partner, cuddling up with a box set, or a family movie night. It's an easy habit to fall into, so whilst I wouldn't go so far as advising a complete*

"digital detox", I would caution you to beware the perils of double screening!

CPD

Continuing Professional Development (CPD) is important for anyone in any job, whether they work from home to not. The difference is, HomeWorkers must generally take charge of their own. This means that as well as progressing through stages of your career and achieving various milestones, you *yourself* have to define what those stages and milestones are. So any professional goals you set should reflect not only the path you hope your career will take but also the ways in which you hope to grow and develop as a professional along the way.

Have a think about what areas of your skillset you'd like to develop or acquire from scratch. These are specific skills that will directly improve how you perform professionally. Perhaps you'd like to learn a new piece of software, or learn to code. Maybe you'd like to learn a new language in order to communicate with foreign clients. If online marketing is required for your business, but it's got you flummoxed, take one of the many courses out there to learn more about it.

This quote, often (but I think erroneously) attributed to Gandhi, sums it up nicely:

LIVE AS IF YOU WERE TO DIE TOMORROW; LEARN AS IF YOU WERE TO LIVE FOREVER.

Some clever soul or other.

Whoever said it was spot on. I'm trying to instil in my children a thirst for knowledge, which I hope will grow into a lifelong passion for learning new things. I think it's more important than academic achievement or exam results (they'll have enough people drumming the importance of *those* into them).

> ***Caution:*** *If like me, you have this passion for learning, it can become the sneaky crack through which the procrastination demons will crawl…so watch out! You'll say to yourself* "Ah, but this is work!" *and think you need to learn what a particular piece of content is teaching before you can get your work done. That's unlikely to be the case. If this sounds like you, limit yourself to watching only one or two TED talks or training videos per day!*

There is always something new to learn, some new skill to acquire. In the world of HomeWorking and running your own business, the list can feel endless and overwhelming. My advice is to always have something on the go to educate yourself: a book, an online course, training manuals, etc. But don't let it take over your whole day. A little learning each day will make you smarter and more fulfilled, both of which will be advantageous to your HomeWork.

How to Feel Successful

So how do you know if you're doing well?

Easy: just check your bank balance, right?!

Well, not quite, no. Obviously, if the "lines are all going up" in your business then that's great. But if you want to measure the complete picture of your home/work/life success, you'll need to use other yardsticks than a balance sheet.

Additionally, I'm afraid the answer rather depends on what parameters you've already set for yourself during your goal setting. But I'd suggest our old friend, regular contentment, should feature highly in your answer.

If you can say at the end of every day that you did most (if not all) of the following things, then I'd say you're living a successful life and doing well in your career:

- I performed all or most of the tasks in my planner for today.
- I exercised.
- I ate well.
- I got closer to achieving what I've set out to do in my personal and/or professional life.
- I earned money from my endeavour.
- I enjoyed at least part of what the endeavour entailed.
- I was aware of my mental wellbeing and took positive steps to maintain it.
- I kept things in perspective.
- I enjoyed my life outside of my work.

Obviously, these things are all about **you**. Of course, there are other considerations I'd include that add up to a valuable existence, like doing things for others, caring for the planet, raising your kids well, showing those around you love and respect.

But this book is about you, and making your HomeWorking life a productive, balanced and happy one!

Takeaways

- Respect your home's primary function as a home.
- Your professional development is your responsibility.
- Always be learning, but don't let it detract from getting things done!

- Define what success looks like for you.

MiniWin

Design a CPD and self-growth timeline that will sit alongside your career goals. Include personal and professional growth targets in your yearly, five-year and ten-year plans.

So the goal categories you'll include in your planner will be:

- Career goals
- CPD
- Personal growth
- Health & wellbeing
- Daily habits

Remember: make them measurable. So "learn how to code," becomes "complete Step 20 of Coding For Beginners course by the end of the year."

Finally, always remember that, unless the act of pursuing a goal contributes directly to your regular contentment, it takes second place to those that do!

12. Conclusion

The world of work will continue to grow and adapt to meet the demands of an ever-changing workforce, our social structures, global pandemics and technological changes. The ability to make your living by working from home may not be new, but never has it been so viable for so many.

It can be pretty amazing, but you have to take it seriously, like any job, and put into practice all the various tactics, tips, boundaries and perspectives we've discussed if you want to make it work for you long-term. You may find you're not the kind of person who can make this work for you. You might spend a week working from home then be *desperate* to get out and interact with colleagues. And that's OK!

But if you *can* find a way to make it work, and your career fits around your home, and your home fits around your work, and they both fit around YOU, then you're on to something special, the golden chalice: not only work/life balance, but home/work/life balance!

I really hope you've found something helpful to chew on in these pages. Now's the time to go through all the notes you made during the MiniWins and start to see the picture of what you want your HomeWorking life to look like come into focus.

I wish you nothing but luck, love, perspective, balance, success and **happiness.**

So get out there — or rather, stay at home — and get to work!

Freebie:

Don't forget to download your FREE copy of
"20 HomeWorking Tips to Supercharge Your Day"

Follow this link to The Happy HomeWorker website:

www.thehappyhomeworker.com/20tips

You'll also find other freebies, blog posts and helpful information all about HomeWorking.

Join The Happy Homeworker Facebook Group

HomeWorkers Of The World Unite!

You work on your own, but you're not alone! More and more of us are embracing HomeWorking, which means more and more of us are discovering its challenges and finding ways to overcome them. By sharing our experience and knowledge, we can help each other to become the best and happiest HomeWorkers we can be.

www.facebook.com/thehappyhomeworker

@thehappyhomeworker on:

Instagram
Pinterest
Youtube

Check out the website:

www.thehappyhomeworker.com

Printed in Great Britain
by Amazon